The New Town and County Hall Series
No. 11

THE GOVERNMENT OF GREATER LONDON

THE GOVERNMENT
OF
GREATER LONDON

BY

S. K. RUCK

Formerly Senior Research Officer, Greater London Group
London School of Economics and Political Science

GERALD RHODES

Senior Research Officer
Greater London Group
London School of Economics and Political Science

LONDON
GEORGE ALLEN & UNWIN LTD
RUSKIN HOUSE MUSEUM STREET

Printed in Great Britain
in 10 *on* 11 *pt Times type*
by Alden & Mowbray Ltd
at the Alden Press, Oxford

PREFACE

On April 1, 1965, far-reaching changes in the government of Greater London came into effect. They were in fact the first major modification to be made in the local government system in this country since it was evolved in the late nineteenth century. We have tried in the following pages not only to describe and give some account of the working of the new system in Greater London, but also to trace its background and interpret its significance. We have also not neglected the fact that there have developed in London separate and in some cases unusual arrangements for the administration of certain services, notably the police, water supply and public transport.

We owe a particularly heavy debt in the preparation of this book to the Greater London Group of the London School of Economics and Political Science, and especially to its Chairman, Professor W. A. Robson, Professor Emeritus of Public Administration. We have both served as Senior Research Officers of the Group and in that capacity have acquired much knowledge of London government. Furthermore, the Group made available to us its extensive and, indeed, unique collection of documentary material relating to London, going back to the Group's own foundation in 1958 as a research body concerned with the governmental problems of London and the South East Region. In particular, we were able to draw on the work done by the Group in its own detailed study of the origins and working of the London Government Act, 1963, the first part of which is to be published in 1970. Without this help, our task would have been immensely more difficult.

We are extremely grateful to two of our colleagues on the Group for finding the time, when L.S.E. was beset by many problems, to read and comment on the manuscript. Dr Roy Parker made many valuable suggestions on Chapter VI and Mr David Regan read the whole of the manuscript and offered many stimulating comments. Needless to say, neither they nor the Group are responsible for the views expressed in these pages.

7

We wish to thank Mr S. D. Askew, Clerk of the Metropolitan Water Board, Mr G. S. Downes of the Metropolitan Police, and Mr R. M. Robbins of the London Transport Board for much valuable information and comment.

Finally, we are grateful to the Controller of Her Majesty's Stationery Office for permission to use certain material from *The Lessons of the London Government Reforms* by the Greater London Group (Royal Commission on Local Government in England, Research Study No. 2, H.M.S.O. 1968); and to the Director-General and Clerk of the Greater London Council for permission to reproduce the map on page 190 from the G.L.C. publication, *Greater London Services.*

G. RHODES
S. K. RUCK

July 1969

CONTENTS

Chapter I

LONDON GOVERNMENT
THE HISTORICAL BACKGROUND

The Lord Mayor of London is probably the best known figure in English local government. Yet despite the pomp and pageantry of the Lord Mayor's Show, the truth is that he presides over a body whose jurisdiction extends to only a small corner of what is now London, and whose powers even within that small corner – the City of London – are comparatively limited. An understanding of this paradox is essential if we are to realise the significance of recent changes in London's government, and, in particular, to appreciate the importance of the existence since April 1, 1965, of a directly elected body responsible for the first time for a number of important matters in the whole area of Greater London – the Greater London Council.

The area of Greater London is defined in the London Government Act, 1963. It stretches from Enfield in the north to Coulsdon in the south, and from Uxbridge in the west to Hornchurch in the east. It covers 622 square miles and contains $7\frac{1}{2}$ million inhabitants.[1] Why was this particular area chosen – and why was it necessary to have a special Act of Parliament dealing only with London government? The purpose of this first chapter is to seek answers to these questions by exploring the historical background. The main theme is the uniqueness of London as its government has developed over the years. This is epitomised in the City of London, a unique survival untouched even by the 1963 Act. But it is also evident in the special arrangements for the administration of the police (the Metropolitan Police), water supply (the Metropolitan Water Board) and public transport (the London Transport Board), all of which will be discussed in more detail later in this book. Above all, the division of powers between the Greater London Council and the London Borough Councils set out in the London Government Act, 1963, represents a new stage in the evolution of English local government.

[1] See map, p. 190.

LONDON GOVERNMENT BEFORE 1888

The City of London has a very long history as a community with its own specific rights and privileges. The first Mayor was appointed in 1192, and by the middle of the fourteenth century a corporate body of Mayor, aldermen and councilmen had been established, the forerunner of the modern Corporation of London.[1] A striking fact about the area of the City is that it has remained almost unchanged since the time of the Norman Conquest. At that time this square mile was London, but in the course of time other settlements grew up adjacent to the City, notably in Westminster and at the south end of London Bridge in Southwark, which the Corporation was authorised to incorporate, although it never did so. By the time of the first Census in 1801, the population of the City was nearly 130,000, but Westminster had over 150,000, Southwark nearly 70,000, and the remaining parts of the continuously built-up area over 500,000.[2] Moreover, only the City had at that date anything which could be regarded as an effective organ of local government. Beyond the City and Westminster, there were the parish vestries and numerous special authorities, each responsible in its own limited area for such functions as street lighting and paving.

This phenomenon of the City remaining within its square mile when all around it a newer and bigger London was growing up is so important to the understanding of the development of London's government that it is worth examining briefly how it came about and what kind of body was responsible for the City's government in the period before and during the nineteenth century reforms of local government which began with the Municipal Corporations Act of 1835.[3]

The City Corporation was a municipal corporation of ancient origin, but it had two important characteristics which made it stand out from other corporations. First, the City was outstandingly wealthy; secondly, although London was the national capital, the seat of government was established not in the City but in neighbouring Westminster. These facts were largely instrumental in the adoption

[1] For a brief account of the origins and early history of the City Corporation, see *The Corporation of London* (Oxford University Press for the Corporation, 1950); also, the City's evidence to the Royal Commission on Local Government in Greater London, 1957–60 (*Written Evidence*, I, pp. 33–48, H.M.S.O., 1962).

[2] See W. A. Robson, *The Government and Misgovernment of London* (London, Allen & Unwin, 2nd edition, 1948) p. 42.

[3] For the constitution and working of the City Corporation in the eighteenth century, see S. and B. Webb *The Manor and the Borough* (London, Longmans, Green, 1908, reprinted, London, Frank Cass, 1963), Chapter X, from which the following is largely derived.

from an early date of a strongly independent position by the City Corporation, and in giving it a particularly important power in relation to the Court and Parliament. As the Webbs put it: 'contributing many times more in money and men than any other local jurisdiction, and actually adjoining the seat of government, it could yet shut its gates against the King and his officers'.[1]

A major result of this situation was that by the eighteenth century the City Corporation had secured that it was almost immune from outside interference in running its own affairs. Furthermore, it could claim certain hard-won privileges; for example, through its Sheriffs it could seek redress of grievances at the Bar of the House of Commons; and it acted as 'a sort of unofficial mouthpiece'[2] for the people of England in criticising government policy.

There was a further interesting fact about the City's government as it had developed by the eighteenth century. Unlike many other municipal corporations of that time it was not a closed body, a self-perpetuating oligarchy intent only on dissipating municipal revenues by feasting and corruption. The City of London had developed a complex constitution which in theory and to some degree in practice also was highly democratic. The basis of this democracy was the fact that the great majority of the resident, rate-paying householders were freemen of the City, and that only freemen were eligible for municipal offices. It is true that becoming a freeman was not perhaps as glorious as it sounds. In order to practise many occupations such as shopkeeper, fruit porter or waterman, it was necessary to be a freeman and this freedom – a mere 'licence to trade'[3] for most of its recipients – was easily purchased, the fees indeed being an important source of the City's revenues.[4] It is also true that these basic facts did not prevent the City's government from being dominated by a relatively small number of important citizens, nor did they prevent 'a great amount of petty corruption and jobbery'[5] in City government. Nevertheless, in comparison with many if not most municipal corporations of the time the City of London was well run.

The two chief bodies responsible for conducting the business of the City were the Court of Aldermen and the Court of Common Council. The former, presided over by the Lord Mayor who was selected as the senior alderman, had twenty-six members, one for each ward of the City, elected for life by the freemen ratepayers. The

1 op. cit., p. 571.
2 ibid, p. 574.
3 ibid, p. 584.
4 Averaging over £6,000 p.a. between 1800 and 1835 (Webbs, op. cit., p. 584).
5 ibid, p. 648.

latter consisted of the Lord Mayor, the other twenty-five aldermen and about 200 common councilmen elected annually by the freemen ratepayers of the wards. For the purpose of this historical background, two points are of interest: (*a*) aldermen, although they had to be freemen, were not necessarily householders or resident in the City; they tended to be elderly and wealthy, were the City's Justices of the Peace, and claimed their main power through judging the validity of all elections to Ward or Corporation offices; (*b*) Common Council became, from the mid-eighteenth century onwards, the main organ of administration, managing the City's property, levying taxes, etc.; it worked through a series of committees with elaborate standing orders; in contrast to the aldermen, common councilmen were mostly tradesmen, shopkeepers, etc., resident in the City.

The officers of the City had many and varied titles such as Salt Shifter, Keeper of the Green Yard and Deputy Oyster Meter. A peculiarity of the City's constitution was that the officers were not chosen by or responsible to a single body. Of the principal officers, for example, the Recorder, the chief legal adviser, was appointed by the Court of Aldermen, and the Town Clerk, the chief of the executive staff, by the Court of Common Council.[1]

With such a background it is not perhaps very surprising that a principal concern of the City Corporation should be with the preservation of its unique and privileged position, which it could scarcely have done if it had extended its boundaries to include Westminster and the other growing areas at the beginning of the nineteenth century. The history of Westminster in particular provides a strong contrast to that of the City.[2] Until the time of Elizabeth, Westminster had a form of manorial government which did not differ greatly from that to be found generally elsewhere in the country. But in 1585, largely at the instigation of Lord Burghley, the Queen's principal minister, Parliament passed an Act creating a special body known as the Court of Burgesses with the power to deal with certain limited classes of offences. The problem was quite simply that the manorial system was inadequate to cope with the problems associated with rapid population growth (e.g. the accumulation of filth in the streets) and yet Westminster's growing importance required some action to be taken. At the same time a really powerful body such as the City Corporation would not have been welcome 'at the gates of the Royal Palace'.[3]

[1] Unusually for the eighteenth century, the Town Clerk was paid a salary and not by fees.

[2] See the Webbs, op. cit., Chapter IV.

[3] ibid, p. 214.

Burghley's compromise solution did not prove an effective answer and by the eighteenth century the government of West-minster was largely in the hands of the Justices of the Peace, together with the parish select vestries which were to be found in most parts of London outside the City.[1] Again in the latter part of the eight-eenth century Westminster acquired a special statutory body, the Westminster Paving Commissioners, to deal with a particularly pressing problem, but this was a solution which was also being tried in many other places. Thus Westminster, unlike the City, did not by the end of the eighteenth century possess any truly effective organ of government. The Court of Burgesses did indeed survive until 1901, but as 'a friendly social gathering'. It was abolished by the London Government Act of 1899, and its property ('a mace, a loving-cup, a snuff-box') was transferred to the new Metropolitan Borough of Westminster.[2] In the contrast between the City and Westminster at the end of the eighteenth century, and indeed between the City and other parts of London, lay the real problem of London government at the time.

This became evident as the growth of London in the late eighteenth and early nineteenth centuries gave rise to difficulties which forced themselves on the attention of Parliament and of public-spirited men. It cannot be too strongly emphasized how remarkable was the posi-tion of London relative to the rest of the country even at this stage. Two aspects are particularly important: first, the population of London was, at the time of the first Census in 1801 about one-tenth of the total population of England and Wales;[3] secondly, London dominated and spread out from one single centre into the surrounding areas. There were never any substantial towns in Middle-sex, Surrey, and the other surrounding counties to challenge London.

These facts, together with the special position of the City referred to above, have coloured the history of London's government right down to our own day. The first serious challenge presented by London's growth which existing arrangements were totally inade-quate to meet was the fundamental one of the preservation of law and order. The City of London had its watchmen, but in the remain-der of the metropolitan area in the eighteenth century 152 separate

---

[1] Close or select vestries were ones in which existing members filled vacancies as they arose by co-option, as opposed to the open vestries whose members were directly elected by the ratepayers.

[2] Webbs, op. cit., p. 231.

[3] That is, if one takes merely the continuous built-up area at that time. For the rates of growth of the *conurbation* area in relation to England and Wales as a whole, see *Report* of the Royal Commission on Local Government in Greater London 1957–60 (Cmnd. 1164, 1960), p. 290.

parishes managed as best they could with the traditional system of parish constables.[1] From about the middle of the century onwards, however, the practical efforts of men like Henry Fielding to institute some kind of rudimentary policing and the deliberations of innumerable Parliamentary committees indicated a growing concern with the problem. Despite the urgency given to these efforts by incidents such as the Gordon riots of 1780, it was not until 1829 that Peel succeeded in getting passed a Metropolitan Police Act which for the first time established an effective police force in London.

There were three outstanding features about the Metropolitan Police which have remained to this day. It was put under the control of the Home Secretary; it was responsible for a very large area and not simply the central built-up part of London;[2] and the City of London was excluded from its jurisdiction.[3] Except for an abortive attempt to model three provincial police forces on the Metropolitan Police pattern,[4] police arrangements in London have remained unique.

The Metropolitan Police might have remained an isolated example, a unique arrangement to meet a particular problem which in London was more acute than elsewhere. Instead, it became the first of many similar approaches to deal with problems piecemeal as they arose. This gave rise to an unco-ordinated system of local government, as happened in much of the country while nineteenth-century local government was being evolved; but it also led to the distinctively different system in London as compared with the rest of the country. This situation would not have arisen had London been treated in the same manner as other large cities and a municipal corporation made responsible for the area of the metropolis. For this to have happened the jurisdiction of the City Corporation would have had to be extended to the whole of London, and its constitution reformed, a course which the Corporation resisted. Moreover, the opportunity for doing so, under the Municipal Corporations Act of 1835, was not taken. That Act followed the first report of the Royal Commission on Municipal Corporations which dealt only incidentally with the

[1] See T. A. Critchley, *A History of Police in England and Wales*, 900–1966 (London, Constable, 1967) p. 30, and for further information on London's policing, see below, Chapter VII.

[2] Originally an area of approximately six to seven miles radius from Charing Cross which was extended in 1839 to twelve to fifteen miles, substantially the same as the Metropolitan Police District today.

[3] Peel claimed that he would be afraid to meddle with the City (see Norman Gash, *Mr Secretary Peel*, London, Longmans, Green, 1961, p. 492). The City has retained its separate police force to this day.

[4] Critchley, op. cit., pp. 86–7.

City of London, since the pressing problems of the time arose from the situation elsewhere. By the time that the Commission, in their second report in 1837, concluded that an extension of the City's jurisdiction was the best solution for London, the impetus for reform was largely spent, particularly as it could only have been achieved against the strong opposition of the City Corporation.

At the same time, the very size and growth of London compelled action to deal with pressing problems, notably in the public health field. As these could not be dealt with on the municipal corporation pattern of places like Liverpool and Birmingham, some other means had to be found. A solution was not arrived at until 1855 when the Metropolis Management Act was passed. The immediate origin of this measure was the Report in 1854 of a Royal Commission on the City Corporation which recommended that the Municipal Corporations Act of 1835 should be applied to the City and that a further seven municipal corporations should be established in the surrounding areas of the metropolis such as Finsbury, Westminster and Southwark. This proposal was rejected by the Government. The Commission also recommended that an indirectly elected board should be set up to carry out drainage and other works of metropolitan significance. This was the proposal which was put into effect by the 1855 Act, under which a Metropolitan Board of Works was established.

The Act was expressly designed to improve the arrangements for sewerage and drainage in London, and for paving, cleansing and lighting the streets. It did this by dividing powers between the existing parishes and the new Metropolitan Board of Works. The area defined as the metropolis contained practically the whole of built-up London at that date.[1] Within it there were ninety-nine parishes. Twenty-three of the largest parishes, including St Pancras and St George's, Hanover Square, continued to be administered by vestries elected by the ratepayers; the remaining parishes were grouped for the purposes of the Act into fifteen districts administered by district boards, whose members were elected by the united vestries of the constituent parishes. The vestries and district boards were responsible for local sewers and drains and other local matters. They also elected the forty-five members of the Metropolitan Board of Works. Of these, three were appointed by the City Corporation, two by each of the six largest vestries, one by each of the other seventeen large vestries, and the remainder by the district boards. One of the Board's

[1] This was fortuitous; the area was not specifically chosen for its purpose, but, as so often, simply taken over from an area which already existed for another purpose—in this case the area used in the eighteenth century for compiling the weekly Bills of Mortality.

B

main tasks was to design and construct a system of main sewers to prevent sewage being discharged into the Thames in London. It also had power to improve the road system and administer building regulations. In course of time it acquired additional functions, being responsible for the building of the Embankment and for the establishment in 1866 of the Metropolitan Fire Brigade, among other activities.

Although the Metropolitan Board of Works was the most important organ of local government in London in the middle years of the century, it was by no means the last of the bodies set up to deal with specific functions; in 1867 the Metropolitan Asylums Board was established; in 1870 the London School Board; and, even as late as 1902, the Metropolitan Water Board.[1] *Ad hoc* arrangements were of course commonly found elsewhere in the middle years of the nineteenth century, but in no other city of the kingdom could be found such a profusion of arrangements with no directly elected body responsible even for the basic local government services.

THE ACTS OF 1888 AND 1899

Under the Local Government Act, 1888, a London County Council was created on the analogy of county councils in the rest of the country; the area was (with a few minor adjustments) that of the Metropolitan Board of Works. It might seem at first sight that this would make London like the rest of the country in its local government structure. This was not so. The 1888 Act was designed to deal with the problem of the predominantly rural counties. The towns had been reformed by the Municipal Corporations Act of 1835 – and by subsequent legislation – whereas local administration outside the boroughs was in the hands either of the justices of the peace in the counties or of various *ad hoc* bodies such as the Boards of Guardians. The 1888 Act substituted elected county councils for the justices in Quarter Sessions as the organ of county government. But London was not a county; it was an urban area of great size which, as has been indicated, had grown up with its own peculiar set of institutions from the City Corporation to the London School Board. How, then did it come to be included in the 1888 Act? The immediate reason was a series of financial scandals involving members of the Metropolitan Board of Works, which focused attention on that body and compelled the Government to seek changes in its constitution. What the 1888 Act did in fact was to transform the indirectly

1 See below, Chapter VII.

elected Board into a directly elected council covering the same area
and with the same functions. From the start, therefore, the London
County Council (L.C.C.) was a misfit. It was not a county – it was
artificially created out of parts of the counties of Middlesex, Surrey
and Kent – and because of its inheritance of the functions of the
Board it did not perform the same role, as, say, the Lancashire
County Council. Once more, therefore, London was given a special
form of government, but not one specifically designed for its particular problems; rather it was an accidental by-product of the reform of
county government.

By 1888, however, London's built-up area already extended beyond
the boundaries of the L.C.C.; this was most noticeable in areas like
West Ham and Tottenham, but it was obvious that in no direction
could the boundary be regarded as having any relevance in terms
not only of London's past growth, but, more importantly, in terms
of the growth which might be expected to take place in the future.
In these adjoining areas the 1888 Act established no less than six
separate authorities,[1] so that the opportunity to create a unified
local government structure for the growing metropolis was lost.

This does not mean that there was no concern with the problems
of London Government in the late nineteenth century; on the con-
trary, there was much discussion and efforts were made to deal with
the problems but they all proved abortive. In 1884, for example,
the Government had introduced a Bill which would have extended
the City's jurisdiction to the whole of the built-up area. In the face
of the Corporation's resistance to this proposal the Government
does not appear to have pursued the matter with any vigour and the
Bill lapsed.

Furthermore, the Act of 1888 left not only the City untouched but
also the vestries; nor were these affected by the Local Government
Act of 1894 which in the rest of the country established a uniform
system of urban and rural districts within the counties. But in that
same year a Royal Commission reported on the Amalgamation of
the City and County of London.[2] It favoured an amalgamation of
the two and at the same time recommended the creation of new
authorities in the County of London to be larger than the vestries
and with greater powers. The latter proposal was carried into effect
by the London Government Act of 1899 under which twenty-eight

[1] West Ham and Croydon county borough councils and the county councils
of Middlesex, Essex, Kent and Surrey.
[2] The City formed part of the area of the County of London for certain
administrative purposes under the Act of 1888 but remained a separate
authority.

Metropolitan Boroughs were established;[1] the proposal to amalgamate the City and County was not put into effect.

With the Act of 1899 London's local government structure was established in the form in which it was to last until 1965. London government was not static in the first part of the twentieth century but the significant developments were not in local government but in the establishment of special bodies to meet particular needs – the Metropolitan Water Board in 1902, the Port of London Authority in 1908, and, most important of all, the London Passenger Transport Board in 1933. These will be considered in Chapter VII.

LONDON 1900 TO 1939

It will be obvious from the brief account given above that the system of local government in London at the beginning of the twentieth century had evolved partly as a result of the particular problems of the metropolis, partly because of the position and attitude of the City Corporation, and partly through historical accident. The result was a curious mixture. Just as London's growth has consisted of successive stages outwards from a single centre,[2] so one could view its local government in terms of concentric rings. In the centre would be the City of London, a unique survival of an earlier age, its electoral system and constitution without parallel anywhere else in the country, its powers a mixture of ancient rights and privileges with modern local government functions,[3] and above all a repository of ceremonial and the outward trappings of local government exemplified in the Lord Mayor's Show and Guildhall banquets. Surrounding the City for distances of three to seven miles were the L.C.C. and the twenty-eight metropolitan boroughs, analogous to a county and municipal boroughs elsewhere, but with a unique division of powers between them, in which the L.C.C. came increasingly to be the dominant partner. Finally, beyond the L.C.C. boundary was the normal local government pattern of county boroughs on the one hand and counties, municipal boroughs, urban districts and rural districts on the other.

It is conceivable that this system, haphazard though its growth had been, might have been adequate to deal with London's problems

[1] The powers of the Metropolitan Boroughs were, however, less than those of boroughs elsewhere in the country, largely because of the special powers of the L.C.C.

[2] London, it is important to note, is not a true conurbation; it has not grown by the coalescing of separate towns but by the outward spread of a single urban centre.

[3] See below, p. 77.

if London had remained as it was in the 1880s. The London County
Council would then have been responsible for the greater part of the
continuous built-up area and it could plausibly have been argued that
it was justifiable to have a local authority with special powers in this
area to deal with the particular problems presented by this unique
concentration of population. Unfortunately for such an argument
London was not static. By 1914, places like Wimbledon, Leyton and
Willesden bordering on the county of London were physically linked
to it and tongues of development ran out to places like Edmonton
on the north and Ealing on the west. Not only were such places
physically part of London, but their inhabitants were dependent on
London very largely for employment and other purposes. Similar
developments were of course taking place round other large towns
and cities in the country. But under the 1888 Act these towns had
been constituted as county boroughs; and as county boroughs they
were generally eager to extend their boundaries with each successive
shift of population outwards, so that the Sheffield or Manchester of
1960 was very much larger in area than the original county borough
of 1889. Such extensions of boundary were not easily won in
the face of opposition from the counties to the loss of valuable
parts of their territory, and the whole question of county borough
extensions loomed large in the difficulties of twentieth-century local
government.

The situation was quite different in London. No major change of
boundary occurred in the area of what is now Greater London[1]
between 1888 and 1965, except for the creation of East Ham as a
county borough in 1915. Yet increasingly there was awareness that
the continuing growth of London was creating problems which were
not confined simply to the county of London. Between 1905 and
1920, for example, four official committees all reached the conclusion
that London's traffic problems required a single authority to be
responsible for traffic and transport services over an area at least as
big as Greater London.

No immediate action followed these recommendations but the
Government were persuaded, mainly as a result of a request of the
L.C.C. itself, to set up a Royal Commission in 1921 to examine the
whole question of local government in 'the administrative county of
London and the surrounding districts'. But the Commission could not
agree on how they should deal with the problem presented to them.
The majority, including the Chairman, Viscount Ullswater, saw

[1] There were, however, numerous changes in the boundaries of county districts, particularly in Middlesex between 1919 and 1939 as a result of the rapid
urbanisation of the county in those years.

their job as being simply to hear the evidence presented to them, and to weigh it up in order to arrive at their conclusions. On this basis, since most of the local authorities did not wish to see their own position changed, these members of the Commission concluded that no major changes in the local government of the area were needed.

There were, however, two minority reports, one of which, signed by two members, advocated far-reaching changes. The main point of disagreement between the minority and the majority concerned the need for action on problems of Greater London as a whole. Apart from traffic and transport, town planning and housing were the main problems presented by London's growth which seemed to need looking at for a wider area than the county of London. The majority of the Commission recommended that a committee should be set up to advise the Minister on these matters, but to the minority this was an inadequate solution and they advocated a directly elected Greater London authority to take responsibility.

The one positive action which followed the Ullswater Commission's Report was the setting up of the London and Home Counties Traffic Advisory Committee in 1924. As its name implies, it had a more limited role than the majority of the Commission had suggested.[1] To deal with questions of town planning, a Greater London Regional Planning Committee was set up in 1927 at the instigation of the Minister of Health; it had representatives of local authorities from the same area as that covered by the Traffic Advisory Committee, but in its very first report the committee questioned whether a body without executive powers could be effective in regional planning. Negatively, the setting up of the London Passenger Transport Board in 1933 might also be seen as a result of the Ullswater Commission, since one reason for creating such a body was that there was no local authority for an area large enough to have made sense in public transport terms.

Local government in the Greater London area thus continued largely unchanged in the twenties and thirties. At the same time, the outward spread of London into the surrounding counties accentuated those problems of traffic and planning which had already begun to be felt in the early years of the century. By 1939 Middlesex was as much an urban county as London had been in 1888. In local government terms the growth of population brought other problems. Boroughs like Ealing were large and populous and were eager to

[1] It covered an area larger than Greater London, but as so often in London's governmental history the reason was largely accidental; a London and Home Counties Electricity District had recently been established and this was used as the basis for the traffic area.

claim the status of county borough – a claim which would have succeeded from an authority with equivalent resources outside the Greater London area. But this presented a dilemma to the Government. If Ealing and similar places in the Greater London area were granted county borough status there would *de facto* be a fundamental change in the local government structure; the county of London, instead of being ringed by a small number of counties which, with the exception of Middlesex, were not wholly urban, would have as neighbours a much larger number of independent authorities, each concerned (as were Croydon, West Ham and East Ham) with only a small part of the whole built-up area. In these circumstances it is not hard to imagine the even greater difficulties which would have arisen in attempts to concert action for Greater London as a whole. Quite apart from this major governmental problem, the claims of places like Ealing and Ilford to county borough status led to tensions within the local government structure. The counties inevitably resisted these claims, and, particularly in Middlesex which saw itself as most threatened, relations between county and ambitious boroughs became strained.

By 1939, therefore, it could be argued that not only had effective governmental machinery not been devised to deal with problems whose origin had been evident even before the Ullswater Commission of the twenties, but also that the solution of those problems in terms of local government structure was yearly becoming more difficult. It was perhaps fitting that in that year there should be published the first full-scale analysis of London's governmental problems by an eminent scholar of the London School of Economics and Political Science.[1] Its author proposed that for certain functions there should be an authority for Greater London as a whole. But there was little sign at that date that the Government were willing seriously to consider making any major changes in London's government.

POST-WAR EVENTS:
THE DECISION TO SET UP A ROYAL COMMISSION

Towards the end of the war of 1939–45 the Coalition Government issued a White Paper on 'Local Government in England and Wales during the Period of Reconstruction'.[2] This proposed among other things that there should be a Local Government Boundary Commission to examine local government areas, particularly in

[1] W. A. Robson, *The Government and Misgovernment of London* (London, Allen & Unwin).
[2] Cmd. 6579 (H.M.S.O., January 1945).

relation to the creation and extension of county boroughs. The Commission was, however, to be specifically excluded from considering applications for county borough status in Middlesex. The White Paper recognised that there was a major problem of whether the boundary of the county of London should be extended, but argued that the time was not right for dealing with it. On the other hand, it was proposed that a separate enquiry should be undertaken into the number, size and boundaries of the metropolitan boroughs and the distribution of functions between them and the L.C.C.

This latter enquiry was duly begun by a committee of five, under the chairmanship of Lord Reading, appointed in April 1945. It had not completed its work, however, when it was wound up by the Government. The main reason given by the Minister of Health (Mr Bevan) for thus terminating its work in October 1946 was that a much wider investigation was needed into the problems of Greater London, but that this could only be undertaken after it had been decided what functions local authorities were to perform.[1] In spite of this the Labour Government of 1945–51 did not undertake any large-scale investigation into London's governmental problems.

The one problem which did receive attention in these years was that of the co-ordination of planning. The war-time Government of Mr Churchill had in 1942 commissioned Professor Abercrombie to prepare a Greater London Plan for an area of 2,600 square miles whose boundaries extended out into Bedfordshire and Buckinghamshire and included the whole of the counties of Surrey and Hertfordshire.[2] When the Abercrombie Plan was produced, one problem confronting the Government was how to ensure that any action taken on it was co-ordinated among the 143 local authorities in the area who exercised planning powers at that time.[3] The then Minister of Town and Country Planning (Mr Silkin) accordingly announced in March 1946 the setting-up of a London Planning Administration Committee under the chairmanship of Mr Clement Davies to consider 'the appropriate machinery for securing concerted action' on a regional plan for London.

This committee reported in 1949 and recommended that there should be an enquiry into London government by a local government commission since they felt that the problem of planning administration could not be adequately dealt with in isolation from

[1] H.C. Deb., Vol. 428, cols. W.A. 1–2, October 24, 1946.
[2] The City and County of London were excluded, each of them producing separate plans.
[3] These were reduced to twelve [by the Town and Country Planning Act, 1947.

other functions. On the immediate issue put to them, a majority of the committee favoured a joint planning committee of the local authorities which would have only limited advisory powers; a minority of members wanted a joint planning board, that is, a body with somewhat greater powers. In the event none of the suggestions of the committee was put into effect by the Government.

One other development was also of significance in this period. This was the extended use of delegation as a feature of county administration. Delegation is an administrative device under which a county council, although remaining responsible for the policy and finances of a particular service, delegates certain powers, especially in day-to-day administration, either to county districts or to some other specially constituted body such as an area board or a divisional executive with representatives both of the county council and of district councils. In particular, delegated powers could, under the Education Act, 1944, be claimed by county districts which had previously exercised elementary education powers (so-called 'Part III authorities'); and delegation was extensively used under the Town and Country Planning Act, 1947.

The position then in 1951 when the Labour Government was defeated in the General Election was that no real progress had been made in tackling problems which affected Greater London as a whole, except to the extent that the Abercrombie Plan provided a framework within which individual local authorities could work. And increasingly during the 1950s it seemed to many people that the problems were likely to increase rather than diminish with the passage of time. To begin with, the continued growth of London began to call in question some of the assumptions on which the Abercrombie Plan had been based. The increase of motor traffic and the accompanying problems of traffic congestion, parking and, more fundamentally, how far one could or should go in attempting to accommodate the motor car in a city like London, provided a most striking example of the need for concerted action, but it was precisely in such fields that administrative responsibilities were most fragmented. Here was scope for a general enquiry into London government, the need for which had been acknowledged but never met by the Labour Governments of 1945–51.

The Conservative Government which took office in 1951 was however, troubled by the perennial problem of ambitious boroughs pressing for county borough status. This was not a problem which was confined to Greater London, but it was made more difficult there because of the Middlesex situation referred to earlier. Ealing and Ilford, both in the area of Greater London, were prominent among the authorities which promoted Private Bills[1] on a number of occasions to achieve county borough status. The Government's invariable answer to such Bills was that it was premature to consider individual promotion in this way until the general question of local government reorganisation had been decided. And in 1954 the then Minister of Housing and Local Government (Mr Harold Macmillan) gave a very guarded promise that something would soon be done on this issue.[2]

The importance of the county borough issue so far as Greater London was concerned was that, as in 1945, it raised the whole question of the future of Middlesex as a county, a question which it seemed difficult if not impossible to resolve without an enquiry into Greater London's government as a whole. The general problem of local government reorganisation was tackled by Mr Duncan Sandys, Mr Macmillan's successor as Minister of Housing and Local Government, by means of lengthy discussions with the local authority associations to try to see how much common ground there was between them. The results of these discussions were embodied in a series of White Papers published in 1956 and 1957, the main proposal being that a Local Government Commission should be established to examine the area and status of local authorities.

London was, however, to be treated differently. Here, the proposals were similar to those put forward in 1945. There were to be no county boroughs in Middlesex; and changes in the County of London 'would have to be specially considered'. The proposed Local Government Commission would, however, be entitled to make recommendations on matters affecting Greater London as a whole.[3]

In January 1957, Mr Henry Brooke succeeded Mr Sandys as Minister of Housing and Local Government, and on July 29 the House of Commons was invited to take note of the three White Papers which had resulted from the Sandys discussions. Mr Brooke departed from the White Papers in one important respect. He announced that the Government had decided to appoint a Royal Commission to examine local government in Greater London. He gave two reasons for this unexpected decision: first, that it did not make sense to exclude the County of London from the investigations

[1] Following the abolition of the Local Government Boundary Commission in 1949 the only means open to a borough seeking county borough status was to promote a Private Bill in Parliament.

[2] Speaking on the second reading of the Luton Bill (H.C. Deb., Vol. 525, col. 712, March 18, 1954).

[3] 'Areas and Status of Local Authorities in England and Wales' (Cmd. 9831, H.M.S.O., 1956), paras. 44–7.

of the Local Government Commission; secondly, that the Middlesex position needed to be examined in the context of Greater London as a whole.[1]

The Report of the Royal Commission which was duly set up under the chairmanship of Sir Edwin Herbert (now Lord Tangley) was an important factor in the establishment of the new structure of local government embodied in the London Government Act of 1963, as will be indicated in the next chapter.

[1] H.C. Deb., Vol. 574, col. 917, July 29, 1957.

Chapter II

THE ROYAL COMMISSION ON LOCAL GOVERNMENT IN GREATER LONDON 1957–1960

The Herbert Commission was formally appointed in December 1957, with the following terms of reference:

'To examine the present system and working of local government in the Greater London area; to recommend whether any, and if so what, changes in the local government structure and the distribution of local authority functions in the area, or in any part of it, would better secure effective and convenient local government; and to regard, for these purposes, local government as not including the administration of police, or of water, and the Greater London area as comprising the Metropolitan Police District together with the City of London, the Boroughs of Dartford, Romford and Watford, the Urban Districts of Caterham and Warlingham, Chorley Wood, Hornchurch, Rickmansworth, and Walton and Weybridge, and the Parish of Watford Rural in the Watford Rural District.'

There are several points of interest about these terms of reference and about the appointment of the Commission. In the first place, the Commission were given the opportunity to carry out a thorough enquiry into the structure and functions of local government in London; the words 'effective and convenient local government' in particular left very wide scope. But, secondly, the functions with which the Commission could concern themselves were strictly limited to those which were actually being performed by local authorities in the area. Police powers, which for the most part were exercised by the Metropolitan Police, and water supply, which was the responsibility of the Metropolitan Water Board in a large part of the area and by private companies in the remainder, were specifically excluded. Public transport, which in many parts of the country is a municipal enterprise, was not mentioned in the terms of reference, and was automatically excluded since no local authorities in the area exercised powers in this field.

No doubt the Government felt that there would be quite enough for the Commission to do in examining existing local authority functions, and certainly a consideration of the Metropolitan Police, for example, would have raised some difficult issues. Nevertheless, these limitations did mean that in dealing with some questions, notably the traffic problem, the Commission had to leave aside some important and relevant considerations.

The third point about the terms of reference is that the area chosen for review was unique. It included the whole of the Metropolitan Police District, an area which had remained practically unchanged since 1839, and which was essentially the area used to define the Greater London Conurbation for statistical purposes (e.g. in the population census); but in addition, a number of other areas were included, particularly Watford and areas adjacent to it. The main object seems to have been to include all those areas which could conceivably be regarded as forming part of the continuous built-up area of London, although in some cases (e.g. Waltham Holy Cross in Essex) the connection was tenuous. By and large, the inner edge of the Green Belt was taken as the boundary.[1]

The membership of the Royal Commission was small, consisting of seven people. Neither the Chairman, Sir Edwin Herbert, nor the other members had any direct experience of local government in London. But two members (Mr Paul Cadbury and Sir Charles Morris) had served as members of provincial local authorities, and another (Sir John Wrigley) had spent the greater part of his civil service career dealing with local government matters. The other members were Miss A. C. Johnston, Mr W. H. Lawson and Professor W. J. M. Mackenzie.

EVIDENCE PRESENTED TO THE COMMISSION

The Commission were presented with a great mass of evidence, particularly from the local authorities in the area. There were 117 of them and all but a few put in written evidence and were examined at oral hearings of the Commission. The government departments with local government responsibilities, the political parties and many professional bodies such as the Town Planning Institute all contributed their quota of information and guidance to the Commission. But in addition to these normal sources of information for a Royal Commission, the Herbert Commission went out of their way to get help, believing, as they said, that 'it was our duty to inform ourselves of the problems of the government of London by all means

[1] See Map 3 (The Growth of London) in *Report* of the Commission (Cmnd. 1164, 1960).

available to us'.[1] Prominent among those means were informal visits to a large number of authorities, but they also commissioned a number of special enquiries. Even more interesting was the approach made by Sir Edwin Herbert early in 1958 to the universities to see whether they were doing any work which might help the Commission's enquiries. This in fact stimulated two important pieces of research by groups of scholars based on London University: one was the Greater London Group of the London School of Economics and Political Science, under the chairmanship of the Professor of Public Administration, W. A. Robson; the other the Centre for Urban Studies based on University College under the chairmanship of Sir William (now Lord) Holford.

The Commission thus cast their net widely. They lacked neither opinions nor information on the problems of London's government. We must next consider what bearing they thought that these problems had on the structure of local government. For most of the local authorities in the Commission's area the existing system was satisfactory. True, some of them wanted increased powers but they did not see this as an occasion for a wholesale revision of areas, functions and status. Rather what they wanted was much more immediate and localised – often county borough status or as near as they could get to it. Typical of those who saw no necessity for change was the London County Council which argued that no greater efficiency would be secured by any alteration in the administration of its area.[2] Typical of those who wanted increased powers but within the existing system were the large boroughs of Middlesex such as Enfield and Harrow.

In sharp contrast to these views was the opinion of the Ministry of Transport and Civil Aviation. For example, on traffic problems they stated quite categorically that 'the multiplicity of authorities concerned and the fragmentation of responsibility for traffic control . . . makes it impossible to deal efficiently with present-day problems'.[3] They therefore thought that there should be some kind of body with powers in this field for the whole of Greater London, although they were less definite about what form this should take.[4] The Ministry of Housing and Local Government too, though more circumspectly, did not find the existing arrangements ideal. They

[1] *Report* of the Royal Commission on Local Government in Greater London (Cmnd. 1164, H.M.S.O., 1960), para. 12.

[2] *Written Evidence* to Royal Commission (H.M.S.O., 1962), Vol. I, p. 27.

[3] *Memoranda of Evidence from Government Departments* (H.M.S.O., 1959), p. 166.

[4] It might be a Council for Greater London, or simply a co-ordinating body, or a separate executive agency.

recognised that the job of trying to find homes and work for Londoners outside Greater London in new and expanded towns required bigger resources than most of the existing authorities possessed; and they drew attention to the advantages of having a single authority to be responsible for a strategic plan for Greater London.[1]

These differences of approach marked a contrast between those who looked only at their own corner of London, whether large as in the case of the L.C.C. or small as in the case of Harrow or Ilford, and those who tried to look at the whole. That the Commission quickly realised the significance of this for their whole enquiry is shown by the amount of attention they devoted at the oral hearings to questions which affected the whole of Greater London such as traffic and overall planning. They asked all the counties and county boroughs, for example, how they thought that a revision of the Abercrombie plan of 1944 should be carried out, given that social and economic changes since the war might have affected the presuppositions on which Abercrombie had worked. Their answers, with one exception, followed the views of the London County Council that 'the present system is the right system because the co-ordinating centre, both for town planning and for transport, is the Government departments'.[2] In other words, these authorities did not regard the initiative in these important matters as being in local government hands; they were quite content to leave it to the ministries. Only Surrey County Council argued differently and thought that there should be a joint planning committee of the authorities in the London area, but this was to be an advisory body only.[3]

On other functions, the Commission received a good deal of information about how existing arrangements worked and of the disadvantages seen by some authorities, but it was not always so obvious why difficulties should have arisen. Education was an example. The Ministry of Education asserted: 'There is no part of the area in which the present system of education administration does not work at least tolerably well.'[4] Yet many of the large boroughs in Middlesex complained that the system had great disadvantages from their point of view. They disliked the system of delegation of education powers as practised in Middlesex. They found particularly irksome the detailed financial control exercised by the county. But what lay behind these boroughs' attitude was the fact that dele-

[1] See Minutes of Evidence, 68th Day, January 12, 1960, Questions 15551 and 15601–2.
[2] Minutes of Evidence, April 23, 1959, Question 2380.
[3] ibid., September 30, 1959, Question 10,450.
[4] *Memoranda of Evidence from Government Departments*, p. 23.

gation brought home to them that they were subordinate to the county whereas their aim was to be independent. The question for the Commission was whether these strained relations between authorities implied that there should be changes in the structure of local government.

Apart from the local authorities and the central departments, the Commission received evidence from a variety of other sources. Among political parties, the London Municipal Society, the local organisation for Conservatives in the County of London, advocated a Greater London authority for a limited range of functions with most-purpose boroughs to perform the remainder with populations of around 250,000. The London Labour Party, on the other hand, followed the L.C.C. in stressing the need for 'respecting the integrity of long established local government units.'[1] The London Liberal Party confined itself to arguing for the introduction of the single transferable vote system.

From professional bodies such as the Town Planning Institute and the Town and Country Planning Association the Commission received evidence that in the planning field at least there was need for fundamental changes; overall planning in their view should cover a larger area than that of any existing local authority or indeed than that which the Commission had been given to review. It was striking how these views recurred in the evidence of other bodies with a professional interest in planning, such as the Royal Institute of British Architects and the Royal Institution of Chartered Surveyors, although they were by no means agreed about the right solution to the problem.

But on the whole the professional bodies, like the majority of local authorities, did not seek great changes in the system of local government. The London Teachers' Association was characteristic of such bodies in arguing, like the L.C.C., that it would be disastrous to break up something which was working well.

It was therefore perhaps of particular interest to the Commission to have the contrasting views of the two university groups which gave evidence. The Centre for Urban Studies did not want to see any radical changes, and put forward data to show that the L.C.C area in particular had a distinct social identity. The Greater London Group, on the other hand, in a lengthy report argued that quite drastic changes were needed if the shortcomings in the existing system were to be overcome. The shortcomings included not only familiar difficulties in planning and traffic, but also the fact that 'There is at present no democratic or representative organ which can both express

[1] *Written Evidence* of Local Authorities, etc. (H.M.S.O., 1962), Vol. 5, p. 253.

and develop the latent consciousness among Londoners ... of belonging to a great metropolitan community'.[1]

From this analysis the Group put forward the view that there should be an elected Greater London Authority to be responsible for such functions as overall planning, main drainage, overspill housing, refuse disposal, major highways and technical education. It was not a new view, but the Group backed it with a great deal of detailed research material. For the remaining local government functions, such as education, housing, the personal health and welfare services, and refuse collection, the Group proposed a new set of authorities. They suggested two possibilities here: one was for about twenty-five boroughs with populations of between 250,000 and 500,000; the other for a small number (six or seven) of counties with populations of about 1 million to $1\frac{1}{2}$ million.

THE COMMISSION'S GENERAL CONCLUSIONS

After considering the great mass of evidence presented to them the Commission came down strongly in favour of change. They argued the need for a Greater London Authority; and for functions which did not require to be performed on a Greater London scale they proposed that there should be established Greater London boroughs. These authorities were to have populations of between 100,000 and 250,000; fifty-two of them were provisionally identified by the Commission, most of them being formed by the amalgamation of existing county boroughs, municipal and metropolitan boroughs and urban districts.

Under the Commission's proposals, therefore, two counties (London and Middlesex) were to disappear entirely, three other counties were to be severely reduced in size (Essex, Kent and Surrey)[2] and the remaining ninety-five authorities within the boundaries of Greater London as defined by the Commission[3] were to be formed into a new kind of 'most-purpose' authority. No official enquiry had argued in detail for a wholesale reorganisation of areas, status and functions on this scale since the local government system had been established in the late nineteenth century. Moreover, much of what they advocated was carried into effect by the London Government Act, 1963. It is important, therefore, to examine the arguments

[1] *Written Evidence*, Vol. 5, p. 446.
[2] Hertfordshire was also slightly affected.
[3] They excluded a number of areas (mainly Watford and surrounding districts in Hertfordshire) from the original review area on the grounds that they did not form part of Greater London.

C

which they put forward in their 250-page report published in October 1960, just under three years after their appointment.

The Report was unanimous, thus contrasting sharply with the Ullswater Commission's Report of the 1920s, the only previous large-scale examination of London's local government. The Commission's general conclusion was that there were some functions which could not be satisfactorily carried out under the existing system; moreover, the system did not give adequate scope for the development of a healthy local government. On both scores, therefore, they felt that a reorganisation of local government was necessary.

These two complementary views of the Commission are clearly brought out in their general discussion of the nature and purpose of local government. After drawing an analogy between local government and a living organism, they concluded:

'Local government is with us an instance of democracy at work, and no amount of potential administrative efficiency could make up for the loss of active participation in the work by capable, public spirited people elected by, responsible to, and in touch with those who elect them.'[1]

This, then, is one important element in the Commission's thinking. At the same time they stressed that they did not believe in change for the sake of change; they recognised that 'the difficulties of local government in Greater London stem more from the complication of the problems to be solved than from inadequacies in the machinery of government'.[2]

NEW AUTHORITIES AND THEIR FUNCTIONS

The heart of the Commission's analysis of the need for fundamental change is to be found in the chapters devoted to Town and Country Planning and to Traffic. In the planning chapter they drew on a background historical discussion to establish the inadequacy of existing administrative arrangements for drawing up and keeping under review a plan for Greater London. They then argued that social and economic changes since the war had called in question many of the assumptions on which existing plans, and in particular the Abercrombie Plan, had been based. They concluded from this that only a body with the statutory duty of examining and planning

---

[1] *Report* (Cmnd. 1164, H.M.S.O., 1960), para. 220.
[2] ibid., paras. 286–7.

for Greater London as a whole could deal adequately with the problem. Given the importance of town and country planning and its close relation to other functions of local authorities, such as highways and housing, it was right that this body should be within local government and not, as so many of the counties and county boroughs had argued in evidence, a part of the central government machinery.

Here, then, is a clear example of the Commission's concluding that a job which needed to be done could not be done without some change in local government structure. In their chapter on Traffic, in which they dealt not only with traffic management but also with the planning, construction, maintenance and lighting of roads, they also found severe limitations in the system as it existed for doing what needed to be done. For example, they described the machinery of government for dealing with these functions as 'chaotic, inefficient and totally out of date'.[1] Largely this was because over the course of time there had developed piecemeal a system of different authorities with different powers, so that, as in the case of traffic management, the result was 'a jumble of *ad hoc* provisions'[2] designed 'to help paper over the cracks in the administrative structure'. They gave examples to illustrate the ineffectiveness of the system, but it is important to note that they themselves stressed that changes in the administrative structure would not necessarily solve London's problems in the traffic field. They did, however, conclude that the problems were insoluble with the existing machinery.

From their analysis, with its emphasis on the variety of authorities with powers in this field, it is not surprising that the remedy suggested by the Commission was that there should be a single authority responsible for traffic management throughout Greater London and also for the construction and maintenance of main roads. This authority, they believed, should be the same as the body they had recommended to be the major planning authority for Greater London, since highway planning was so closely bound up with town and country planning.[3]

If then, as the Commission believed, a Greater London authority was needed, primarily to deal with problems of land use and highway planning, traffic management and overspill housing – functions which had close connections with each other – two major problems had to be faced. First, what sort of authority should this be; secondly, what sort of local government structure was implied for the performance

[1] *Report*, para. 405.
[2] ibid., para. 427.
[3] ibid., para. 442.

of other functions. On the first point the Commission were quite clear that the only possible solution was to have a Council for Greater London as a unit of local government. They rejected as inadequate proposals for joint arrangements between existing authorities or for the establishment of an *ad hoc* planning body. More significantly, they thought that it would be quite wrong to leave these matters to be settled by central government. To do so would be a denial of their faith in local government. As they said in probably the best-known passage of their report:

'we are convinced that the choice before local government in Greater London is, in truth, to abdicate in favour of central government, or to reform so as to be equipped to deal with present-day problems. There are great and growing problems to be solved and the present machinery of local government is inadequate to solve them. Unless this machinery is made adequate, the problems are so great and obtrude themselves so obviously on public attention that they will be taken out of the hands of local government.'[1]

Much the most important part of this attempt to make the machinery adequate was the proposal to set up a Council for Greater London.

Nevertheless, a great many of the services provided by local government did not, in the Commission's view, require to be administered by an authority responsible for the whole of Greater London. Foremost among these were the social services – personal health, welfare and children's services. Here, the Commission's analysis was rather different from their discussion of planning and traffic; they were concerned not so much with the question of whether the existing system was a hindrance to the effective performance of functions, as with the question of what kind of authority and particularly what size of authority was likely to be best fitted to provide a good service. In terms of functional performance they seem to have been particularly influenced by the ideal organisation, suggested to them by the Ministry of Health, for the health and welfare services of 'a team of domiciliary attendants (doctors, nurses, midwives, health visitors and home helps), in which the lead is necessarily taken by the family doctor.'[2] They concluded that a minimum population of 100,000 was desirable if this ideal was to be at all feasible, but they also thought that authorities with more than about 200,000 population would find increasing difficulty in performing thse functions effectively.

As was suggested above, the Commission were not merely

[1] ibid., para. 707.
[2] Ministry of Health *Written Evidence*, para. 50, quoted in *Report*, para. 595.

concerned with effective performance of functions in a narrow sense. They constantly stressed in their report their concern with the health of local government. Before considering what precisely they meant by this and how their view affected their conclusions, it is interesting to see how they applied the idea to the analysis of education, which they themselves called 'the most important of all local authority functions'.[1] Education was at that time the responsibility of the counties and county boroughs in the Commission's area, with the complication that in the counties except London many of the larger county districts had certain delegated powers, a situation which, as has been suggested, had given rise in Middlesex to a good deal of friction between the county and those districts which wished to become county boroughs. The Commission posed seven questions 'to see whether the objects of the Act of 1944 are being attained in Greater London'.[2] Significantly, on only one point did they think that there were serious disadvantages in the existing system, and that was the answer to the question 'is the present system healthy for local government?'

On this they took the view that responsibility for education was a most significant factor in ensuring 'a persistence of lively health' in the boroughs of Greater London; furthermore, it could contribute to arresting 'the withering process in London local government' which much concerned them.[3] Thus in the case of education their view of what constituted healthy local government, as distinct from what they saw as the functional needs of education, was the most important reason leading them to advocate education powers for the smaller authorities – the boroughs of 100,000 population and more. Nevertheless, they did not suggest that the boroughs should, like county boroughs, have exclusive educational powers. They recognised that educational planning required a bigger area, and therefore proposed that the Council for Greater London should have the responsibility for this and the boroughs responsibility for day-to-day administration. What they suggested for education as a whole therefore derived from both functional and healthy local government arguments.

From their recommendations on education and from their more general discussion of local government it is evident that one of their chief concerns was to ensure that a reorganised local government should be able to attract people of ability to serve both as councillors and as officials. This in their view meant primarily two

[1] *Report*, para. 443.
[2] ibid., para. 499.
[3] ibid., para. 518.

things: providing them with a worthwhile job to do; and ensuring that they were not too far removed from the people for whom local government services are provided. They therefore aimed to strike a balance between making authorities too small, which would mean that they would be unable to attract sufficient people of ability, and making them too large, which would lead to remoteness and a lessening of the sense of responsibility.[1]

Thus the Commission's general conclusions can be viewed from two angles. First, there were the jobs which had to be tackled over a wide area and thus logically led to the idea of a Council for Greater London, these were primarily land use and highway planning, but also included traffic management, overall responsibility for education, certain housing powers,[2] the fire and ambulance services, refuse disposal and certain major artistic and sporting centres.[3] Secondly, there were the services which were more truly local, requiring authorities which were not too big and not too small; pre-eminently these were the personal services, personal health and welfare, children and housing (except in the case of the latter for those matters which the Commission thought could only be tackled on a Greater London scale); but they also included a variety of other functions such as refuse collection, libraries, weights and measures, food and drugs legislation and parks and open spaces.

It has already been suggested that the need to keep in mind their twin criteria of administrative efficiency and the health of local government led the Commission to advocate a division of responsibilities in education between the Greater London authority and the local borough authorities. For similar reasons they also proposed a division of responsibilities in a number of other functions, notably planning, highways and, as mentioned above, housing. In planning, for example, although the Council for Greater London was to be responsible for the development plan for the area, the local authorities were to deal with planning applications, subject to certain limitations; in highways, the Council was to be responsible for the planning, construction, maintenance and lighting of main roads, and the local authorities for the remainder.

In presenting their conclusions the Commission drew up a tentative list of their fifty-two proposed Greater London boroughs, ranging in

[1] On these points see especially *Report*, paras. 229–42.

[2] These included the power to build new towns or expand existing towns outside Greater London; and the power to build within Greater London largely to assist those boroughs with particularly difficult housing problems (*Report*, paras. 785–98).

[3] e.g. they suggested that the Royal Festival Hall and the Crystal Palace should be the responsibility of the Council.

size (with one exception[1]) from 81,000 population to 249,000; they were to be formed either from existing local authorities (e.g. Lewisham, Romford) or from amalgamations of existing authorities (e.g. Chelsea with Kensington, Hornsey with Southgate and Wood Green).

These boroughs were to be 'the primary unit of local government in the Greater London area'.[2] In saying this the Commission clearly had in mind their views on the health of local government. It was the boroughs, not the Council, which were to carry the main responsibility for arresting the 'withering process' which they had chiefly found in the lowered status of the existing county districts, deterring people of ability and ambition from standing as councillors.[3] By creating boroughs of sufficient size and resources, with a wide range of important functions, and yet not too large as to make impossible the personal links to which they attached so much importance, the Commission believed that they were laying the foundations for a much improved local government system in Greater London.

Yet there is something paradoxical about this view of the boroughs as the primary unit of local government. For the other part of the Commission's solution for London's problems proposed a powerful authority of a very different kind. Basically, the Council for Greater London was to be an overall planning authority; its decisions were, therefore, bound to have a limiting effect on the boroughs' capacity to act. This was especially true in education, the function which the Commission themselves had called the most important in local government. If then the Council was to do its job effectively, it, rather than the boroughs, would have the primary responsibility in some of the most important spheres of local government activity.

The explanation of the paradox lies in the nature of the enquiry undertaken by the Commission. It has already been pointed out that the main reason compelling the Commission to suggest changes in London's local government was that the problems of planning and traffic could not be resolved under the existing system. The need for a Council for Greater London was in terms of the logic of the argument the first priority for the Commission. But not only did this mean that they were thereby compelled to recast the whole structure of local government in the area; it also meant that the force of events

[1] The exception was the City of London with a resident population of less than 5,000. The Commission conceded that logically the City ought to be amalgamated with Westminster, 'but logic has its limits and the position of the City lies outside them'. It was 'in the national interest' that the City should remain as it was. (*Report*, paras. 935, 943).

[2] *Report*, para. 743.

[3] ibid., para. 688.

was compelling them to recommend an authority which did not fit into their conception of what *local* government should be.

It is true that the Council for Greater London was to be a representative, democratic body and constituted in the same manner as a county council.[1] But although the need for the Council justified far-reaching changes, the Commission saw in the boroughs the true London local authorities of the future.

It was also in keeping with the Commission's general views that they should recommend that the Council for Greater London should have a 'first-class Intelligence Department'. They attached great importance to this, claiming that 'without such a service we do not believe that local government in its traditional sense can continue to exist in London'. They saw it as having a two-fold function: to secure more efficient administration by conducting continuing research into problems affecting Greater London as a whole; and to act as a general clearing house for information serving local and central government and, most importantly, contributing to the growth of an informed public opinion.[2] It was thus to be an instrument of the revitalisation of local government which they regarded as an essential part of their task.

THE COMMISSION'S REPORT AND THE GOVERNMENT'S WHITE PAPER

The Report of the Herbert Commission was described by one observer as 'one of the great state papers of recent years'.[3] It is not hard to see why. It was unanimous; its arguments were presented forcefully and persuasively; it was written in a style refreshingly different from the normal heavy prose of Royal Commission reports. These factors combined to ensure that the case presented by the Commission for fundamental changes received attention. Even those who believed that no more was needed than adjustment of the existing system of local government were compelled to meet the arguments advanced by the Commission, particularly those relating to planning and traffic.

The 104 local authorities directly affected by the proposals of the Commission viewed them with mixed feelings. The counties and county boroughs which were either to disappear altogether or, as

---

[1] *Report*, paras. 850–7.
[2] ibid., paras. 758–63.
[3] D. V. Donnison, *Health, Welfare and Democracy in Greater London* (Greater London Paper No. 5, London School of Economics and Political Science, 1962), p. 5.

with Essex, Kent and Surrey, were to suffer considerable reductions in territory were for the most part strongly opposed to the report. The ninety-five metropolitan and municipal boroughs and urban districts divided almost equally into those in favour and those against it. On the whole, support was strongest in those Middlesex boroughs which had hoped to achieve county borough status and which saw the Commission's proposals for 'most-purpose' boroughs as a great improvement on the existing system. Under these proposals, seven of them would have become Greater London boroughs without having to amalgamate with other authorities. On the other hand, strong opposition to the report came from those metropolitan boroughs (the majority) which were Labour-controlled. In this they took their lead from the Labour L.C.C. which soon emerged as the bitterest opponent of the Herbert Commission's plan.

There were detailed criticisms of the Commission's proposals from professional bodies like the Town Planning Institute who questioned whether the division of functions in planning between the Council for Greater London and the Greater London Boroughs would enable effective action to be taken over comprehensive redevelopment; from bodies like the London Teachers' Association which wanted to retain the existing system of education in the L.C.C. area; and from individuals with an interest in a particular service. Perhaps the strongest criticisms were of the education and planning proposals, the former because it was felt they they would be unlikely to overcome the difficulties associated with the existing system of delegation, the latter because of doubts about whether the proposed division of powers would prove effective in practice. To some degree these criticisms centred on whether the Commission's views on the health of local government had not swayed them too far in the direction of making the boroughs too small for the tasks which had to be performed.

But although there were many detailed criticisms of this kind, the crucial question was whether the general analysis of the situation made by the Commission and their proposals for meeting it were to be accepted. The only serious alternative to the Commission's proposals was put forward by the Surrey County Council, and supported by the other county councils, particularly London and Middlesex.[1] Surrey argued that the Commission had failed to show that the drastic changes which they advocated were really necessary. For strategic planning the area of Greater London was not large enough, and in any case a joint board of the existing authorities

[1] This 'Surrey Plan' was put forward in a printed report *Statement of Views by the Surrey County Council*, dated February, 1961.

was adequate to deal with the problem involved. If this view were accepted, then, as has been shown earlier, a good deal of the argument for completely changing the structure of London's local government would fall to the ground. But there were difficulties in the Surrey view; first, there might be a case for a Greater London plan even within a much larger regional plan; secondly, it was doubtful if a joint board would have effective powers.

It was not until November 1961, over a year after the Herbert Commission had reported, that the Government made known their views. In a White Paper published in that month[1] the Government declared their acceptance of the Commission's criticism of the existing structure of local government, and of their 'broad design' for improving it. This was subject, however, to two important amendments. Clearly the Government, like many of the critics of the Herbert proposals, did not think that the division of powers in education between the Council for Greater London and the boroughs would work well. At the same time they argued that it would be preferable that the boroughs should be larger since they would then be better able with increased resources to develop the services for which they were responsible, and especially to provide more adequately for specialised staff and institutions in the personal services.

From these two arguments derived the two important differences from the Herbert Commission's plan; first, there were to be fewer but larger boroughs (to be known as London boroughs) with minimum populations of about 200,000; secondly, these larger boroughs were to be responsible, like county boroughs, for the whole of education in their areas. There was, however, one exception – and a very important exception – to this plan for education. In the centre of London it was proposed that there should be a single large education authority catering for a population of about 2 million.

The 1961 White Paper is significant for the fact that it represented a Government commitment to a major reform of local government in London, a step which no Government had even contemplated since the system had been devised at the end of the nineteenth century. But nothing better illustrates the difficulties facing such an attempt than the dilemma of education. Education, as the Herbert Commission had recognised, is so important a local government function that its needs must play a large part in shaping the local government structure. In Greater London in 1960 there were only nine local education authorities, although in addition a number of the district councils had a part in the administration. Functional needs seemed to

[1] *London Government: Government Proposals for Reorganisation* (Cmnd. 1562, H.M.S.O., 1961).

point in the direction of fairly large authorities, and in the Commission's scheme this would have been met by the powers proposed for the Council for Greater London; but that scheme also involved an awkward sharing of powers. In rejecting this the Government were faced with the problem of either creating a huge education authority and giving all the powers to the Greater London authority, or of somehow ensuring that the boroughs would be large enough to be able to deal adequately with education.

The proposal in the White Paper seems to be a compromise. Even the enlarged boroughs probably did not satisfy the Ministry of Education's view of the proper size needed for an education authority, and in the centre of London they succeeded in retaining the greater part of the existing L.C.C. area as a single education area.[1] However, the result was to pose further awkward problems. Was there any real justification for having two entirely different systems of educational administration in Greater London? And if there was to be a central area authority why should it not be the whole of the existing L.C.C. area? Undoubtedly, the second question was a very difficult one for the Government since a major reason for restricting the area of the central London Authority was that the case for reorganisation would be weakened if they were forced to admit that the L.C.C.'s educational service should be retained intact. Yet on educational grounds there was undoubtedly a strong case. Since the days of the London School Board of 1870 there had been a single education authority in the L.C.C. area and the education service had been developed as a unity there.

The White Paper left a number of other questions unresolved. But it also signalled the beginning of a period of intense opposition to the proposals. At first this chiefly came from some of the local authorities, particularly the counties, and from a number of professional bodies; but during the course of 1962 the Parliamentary Labour Party came out in direct opposition to any fundamental changes in London's government. This culminated in a pledge by Mr Gaitskell at the end of June that the Labour Party would fight any Bill put forward by the Government on the lines of the White Paper 'clause by clause and line by line'.[2]

Two important changes were made by the Government to their proposals in the spring of 1962. First, nine areas were excluded in

[1] The precise area and nature of the authority were left for further discussion and decision (Cmnd. 1562, paras. 42–3).

[2] For a detailed account of the political struggle, see Frank Smallwood, *Greater London: The Politics of Metropolitan Reform* (New York, The Bobbs-Merrill Company, Inc., 1965).

whole or part from the area of Greater London.[1] Secondly, in May it was announced that the L.C.C. education service was to be preserved intact, but subject to a review after five years. This latter announcement immediately led to demands for the preservation similarly of the L.C.C.'s children service, but the Government were not prepared to concede this.

Particularly bitter opposition to the Government throughout this period came from the L.C.C., culminating in July 1962 in a refusal to co-operate in discussing the necessary preliminary arrangements before legislation could be introduced. Right until the end the L.C.C. seems to have believed that it was inconceivable that the Government would abolish it, claiming that 'for seventy-three years the Council has spoken for the people of London, the capital of Britain, the heart of the Commonwealth: we do not believe that the people of London want that voice silenced.'[2] But was the London of 1962 the same as the London of 1889? This was essentially what the argument was about.

[1] They were Banstead, Caterham and Warlingham, Cheshunt, Esher, Staines, Sunbury-on-Thames, Walton and Weybridge (wholly excluded); Chigwell, Epsom and Ewell (partially excluded).

[2] L.C.C. Minutes, March 12, 1962.

Chapter III

THE LONDON GOVERNMENT ACT, 1963

At the beginning of the 1962–3 Session of Parliament the Queen's speech duly announced that there would be legislation to deal with London government, and the London Government Bill was published on November 20. *The Times* said accurately enough of the Bill that: 'it stakes out the main legislative battlefield for this session'.[1] Largely, this was because the Labour Party Opposition were convinced that a scheme of reform was unnecessary and particularly a scheme which involved the abolition of the L.C.C. In the proceedings on the Bill the Opposition argued strongly, though without success, for the preservation intact of other services of the L.C.C. on the lines provided in the Bill for education.[2]

There were, however, other reasons why the Bill proved to be controversial. It was, to begin with, necessarily a very complex measure; the unique local government structure and functions which were proposed involved a complete recasting of existing legislation so far as it related to London's local government, and left much scope for debate about how powers should be divided between the Greater London Council, the London boroughs and the central departments. Even within the general lines of the Government's scheme there was room for argument on many of these points, and this was intensified by those who sought to make either the G.L.C. or the boroughs stronger. There was, for example, much discussion on whether the G.L.C. had been given adequate powers in the traffic and planning fields as compared with the other authorities.

Apart from these fundamental questions, the Bill also provided the opportunity for argument over matters which had already been much discussed. The precise groupings of existing authorities to form the new boroughs, for example, or whether certain authorities should be

---

[1] *Times*, November 23, 1962.
[2] For an account of these proceedings, see Gerald Rhodes, *The Government of London: The Struggle for Reform* (London: Weidenfeld & Nicolson, 1970), Chapter 10.

excluded from Greater London altogether had been the subject of much negotiation during the earlier part of 1962 and were also debated on the Bill. Questions such as the number of councillors for the new authorities, or whether there ought to be aldermen; of the arrangements for giving financial assistance to the counties which were to suffer loss of territory; or of the areas and composition of the new Executive Councils for National Health Service work – all these gave rise to differences of opinion and had to be resolved before the Bill became law.

It is not therefore surprising that over 1,000 amendments were put down to the Bill, and that a great deal of Parliamentary time was spent on it from December 10, 1962, when the Second Reading debate began until July 31, 1963, when it received the Royal Assent. The first clause and the First Schedule which dealt with the constitution of the new boroughs, were taken in Committee of the whole House of Commons in view of their fundamental importance to the whole Bill. This stage took over twenty-seven hours of Parliamentary time, and led the Government to impose the 'Guillotine',[1] a procedure which because of its unpopularity is resorted to comparatively rarely. There followed twenty-one Sessions in Standing Committee on the remainder of the Bill. There were similar lengthy debates when the Bill eventually reached the House of Lords.

As might be expected, the result of this intense Parliamentary activity was that the Bill received a considerable number of amendments. The purpose of the following pages is to describe the main features of the Act which became law in 1963 as the London Government Act, and which is the basis of London's local government today.

THE NEW AUTHORITIES

The Act lists[2] the composition of the London boroughs, but does not name them.[3] There are thirty-two boroughs altogether.[4] The first elections to them were to be held in May 1964, but they would not take over their new functions until April 1, 1965, thus allowing a period of eleven months during which the new and the old authorities were to exist side by side.

[1] Strictly speaking, this is a motion introduced by the Government for the allocation of time on a Bill or parts of it.

[2] Schedule 1.

[3] The names were determined by the Minister following recommendations by joint committees of constituent authorities (see p. 70).

[4] The City of London is not a London borough, although it has the powers of a London borough in addition to the powers which it possessed before.

The administrative area of Greater London for which a Greater
London Council was to be established was defined as the area of the
London boroughs, the City and the Temples. Unlike the boroughs,
however, the G.L.C. was given the power to change its name with the
consent of the Minister. The first election to the G.L.C. was to be
held on April 9, 1964, thus giving the new authority practically a
year before it took over its responsibilities on April 1, 1965, from
which date all existing authorities including the London and Middlesex[1] county councils and the county boroughs of East Ham, West
Ham and Croydon were to disappear.

Special provision was made in the Act for the constitution of the
Greater London Council, since it is a quite distinctive type of authority, whereas the boroughs are in their essential features similar to
boroughs elsewhere. Among other things, the Council was to have
100 councillors, fewer than the L.C.C. alone had had under the previous system.[2] The number of aldermen was fixed at one-sixth of the
number of councillors, the same ratio as had applied to the L.C.C.,
whereas in the rest of the country the ratio is one-third. Councillors
were to be elected for three years, as is usual in local government,
and to retire simultaneously in 1967 and every third year subsequently, i.e. in the manner of county councillors, although the day of
election was ultimately to be the same day as that fixed for the election of borough councillors in the rest of the country. For the 1964
election the Act specified that the areas of the London boroughs
should form the electoral districts, each borough returning two,
three, or four councillors; the intention was, however, that there
should be single-member electoral divisions in future.[3]

Although the London boroughs were to be in most respects similar
to municipal boroughs elsewhere, some important exceptions were
made. In particular, the number of aldermen was, as in the case of the
G.L.C., to be one-sixth of the number of councillors, and, again as
in the G.L.C., all the councillors were to be elected simultaneously,
instead of one-third being elected annually as in the case of boroughs
elsewhere.[4] The effect would be that both G.L.C. and borough

[1] The Act provided that three urban districts in Middlesex which were excluded
from Greater London altogether should be transferred, Potters Bar to Hertfordshire, and Staines and Sunbury-on-Thames to Surrey (Section 3(1) (c) and (d)).

[2] This was one of the matters which was strongly disputed in the proceedings
on the Bill.

[3] This may operate for the first time in 1973 after the Parliamentary constituency boundaries have been revised to take account of the new London borough
boundaries; G.L.C. electoral divisions will then coincide with constituencies.

[4] London Government Act, 1963, Sch. 4, para. 8 (subsequently referred to as
'1963 Act').

councillors would be elected in 1964, and that all would come up for re-election in 1967.[1]

Behind these arrangements lay an interesting divergence of view. On the one side are those who argue that annual elections of a proportion of councillors help to sustain public interest as well as providing continuity of membership in a council. On the other side are those who argue that, especially with the increasingly party political nature of local government elections, it is right that the electors should be able to pass judgment on the policies the council has been pursuing as a whole in the manner of a Parliamentary general election. Furthermore, it is argued, too many elections are confusing to the voters. The latter point was one which was endorsed by the Herbert Commission who wanted G.L.C. and borough elections to be held on the same day, although they did not make it clear whether they favoured for the boroughs, as they certainly did for the G.L.C., the entire council being elected at the same time.[2]

It will be noticed, however, that the Government did not use the occasion of the reorganisation of London government to deal with two other controversial issues, whether there should be any aldermen on an authority, and whether some or all of the members of an authority should receive payment. On both these questions the Government followed the Herbert Commission in not wishing to treat London differently from the rest of the country, even though they were prepared to retain the special London *proportion* of aldermen. Both questions, but especially the question of payment for councillors, were extensively debated during the passage of the London Government Bill through Parliament.[3]

There are a number of provisions about the general relations between the G.L.C. and the boroughs. These include a power for the G.L.C. to delegate any of its functions by agreement to a borough council,[4] and arrangements for proposing alterations to the boundary of Greater London.[5] The G.L.C. also has power to promote a Bill in Parliament 'for any purpose which is for the public benefit of the inhabitants of Greater London or of any part thereof', and it can do

[1] Subsequently, the Government of the day postponed the borough elections of 1967 to 1968 (see London Government Act, 1967), largely at the request of the London Boroughs Association, although it was alleged by the Conservative opposition that the object was to avoid almost certain heavy electoral defeats.

[2] See *Report*, paras. 854–8.

[3] See in particular *House of Commons Debates*, Vol. 675, cols. 87–99, April 1, 1963.

[4] Section 5(1): this provision is, however, hedged about with a number of restrictions.

[5] Section 6(2) (a).

so at the request of a London borough, and can even propose an alteration in the functions of a borough or the City, after consultation with them.[1]

The London boroughs can themselves make proposals for the alteration of boundaries between them, and there is also an interesting provision that at any time in the five years after the new authorities take over their powers on April 1, 1965, proposals may be made for transferring parts of boroughs on the outer boundary of Greater London to the adjoining counties; these proposals must be made by at least 300 local government electors in the area proposed to be transferred.[2] These, like other proposals for boundary alterations, have to be made to the Minister who then orders a public enquiry. Following approaches made in this way largely by the authorities concerned, enquiries were held into a number of proposals of a relatively minor nature in 1966 and 1967. As a result, the Minister agreed that as from April 1, 1969, the village of Knockholt should be transferred from Bromley L.B. to Kent, and the village of Farleigh and part of Hooley from Croydon L.B. to Surrey.

In considering the provisions in the Act relating to the performance of functions by the different authorities, it has to be remembered that much important detail is contained not in the Act itself but in Regulations made by Ministers. In the following account the more important of these powers will be referred to as well as those set out in the Act itself.

ROAD TRAFFIC, HIGHWAYS AND MOTOR VEHICLES

This is the heading in the Act and it reflects one of the main preoccupations of the Herbert Commission in their analysis of the London situation. Their view of the traffic problem had been that the only solution was for the Greater London Council to have responsibility for traffic management on all roads in Greater London; by traffic management they intended all those measures designed to make easier the movement of people and vehicles through the streets.[3]

The powers laid down in the Act did not deal with the situation quite so simply. This was largely because although the G.L.C. was given the power to make orders for controlling traffic the Minister of Transport also retained certain powers in this field. The original

[1] Section 7 (1) and (2).

[2] Section 6(4): the 300 must constitute at least 10 per cent of the total number of electors in the area.

[3] *Report*, para. 779; the measures include waiting restrictions on vehicles in the streets, designation of one-way streets and provision of traffic lights.

D

Bill presented to Parliament was much criticised because it sought to
retain for the Minister concurrent powers in practically the whole of
the traffic regulation field, whereas the Herbert Commission had
wished to limit his power to that of approving or confirming orders
made by the Council. In the Act as finally passed a compromise was
arrived at, and it was made clear that some important powers of the
Minister (e.g. for revoking an order made by the G.L.C.) were only
to be exercised if the Council was failing to do its duty.[1]

Nevertheless, there remained other restrictions on the G.L.C.'s
power to make traffic orders, the most notable being that they could
not make orders affecting trunk roads without first getting the Minister's consent.[2] In all cases the G.L.C. were to consult with the police
and with any London borough affected before making an order.[3]

By and large, the effect of these statutory provisions was to give
the G.L.C. somewhat wider powers in the making of traffic control
orders than county boroughs in the rest of the country.[4] The important point of change, however, was that there was now to be an
authority locally elected to deal with these matters whereas hitherto
in London only the Minister had had power to make orders.[5]
There was thus to be an extensive handing over of powers from the
minister to the G.L.C. in spite of the fact that in a number of cases
(e.g. fixing speed limits, erecting traffic signs) there remained concurrent powers in this field.

In one important traffic matter, the provision of parking places
whether on or off the street, the G.L.C. was to share powers with the
London boroughs and the City; furthermore, the G.L.C. was not to
exercise its powers without the consent of the borough concerned.[6]
This illustrates the problems posed by the unique local government
arrangements proposed for London. In the rest of the country
county boroughs and county districts exercised this power. Was
London for this purpose to be treated as a single city like Birmingham, or were the local authorities, the boroughs, to have the power
in the same way as municipal boroughs or urban districts? The solution in the London Government Act was to say 'yes' to both ques-

[1] 1963 Act, Section 9(2).

[2] Section 10(1): thus the position as regards trunk roads was to be the same as
in other parts of the country.

[3] Section 10(4).

[4] The Transport Act, 1968, has, however, brought the latter into line with the
G.L.C.

[5] The Metropolitan Police, however, had had power (which was not affected
by the 1963 Act), to make experimental traffic schemes.

[6] 1963 Act, Section 13. Under the Transport (London) Act 1969 the G.L.C.
will have strengthened powers in the traffic field. See below, p. 113.

tions on the grounds that there was both a local parking problem and a problem which arose from the overall traffic situation in Greater London.

Finally, it may be noted in relation to traffic that the Act contained a unique provision requiring the G.L.C. before April 1, 1965, to consult the Minister of Transport about their administrative arrangements for discharging these traffic powers.[1] In itself this indicates both the importance attached to the duty of trying to cope with London's traffic problems, and a certain nervousness on the part of the Ministry about giving up its own powers to a body with no experience of those problems.[2]

The position in relation to the construction, maintenance and lighting of roads in Greater London was rather different. Here the Herbert Commission had proposed quite simply a division into main roads, i.e. those mainly carrying through traffic, and others; the G.L.C. was to have responsibility for the former and the boroughs for the latter.[3] The Act in practice did this with the important exception that responsibility for trunk roads was retained by the Ministry of Transport. The roads for which the G.L.C. was to have responsibility were to be known as 'metropolitan roads'; a list of them was contained in the Act with provision for modifying and adding to the list.[4] There was no specified criterion of what was to constitute a metropolitan road, but they were in fact mainly the more important traffic-carrying roads other than trunk roads most of them being Class I or 'A' roads. There was specific provision in the Act for the G.L.C. to delegate its functions to the boroughs and the City, the object being that the boroughs should act as agents and thus avoid the need for the G.L.C. to set up an elaborate road works department.[5]

The more fundamental responsibility for planning the road system of London as a whole in its broad outlines also belongs to the G.L.C. but may be more conveniently considered below in relation to planning powers.

Finally, it may be noted that the Act made the G.L.C. the authority for vehicle and driving licence purposes which elsewhere are the responsibility of counties and county boroughs.

To sum up the position in the traffic field the legislation recognised

[1] ibid., Section 9(3).

[2] In the original Bill it was specifically provided that the G.L.C. should appoint a director of traffic but this was withdrawn after criticism that it was an undue limitation on the G.L.C.'s powers.

[3] *Report*, paras. 780–1.

[4] 1963 Act, Section 17 and Schedule 7.

[5] ibid., Section 18.

the need for a single powerful authority; in the highways field an attempt was made to meet the view that a distinction can be made between roads which serve mainly local purposes and those which have much wider importance.

HOUSING

The Herbert Commission and the Government in the White Paper had both accepted that housing should be basically a borough function. There were, however, difficulties about making the boroughs the sole housing authorities and these difficulties derived partly from the housing situation in London and partly from the special position which the London County Council held in the existing system. To take the latter first: county borough and county district councils are the housing authorities in England and Wales outside London. But in the L.C.C. area before the 1963 Act both the L.C.C. and the metropolitan boroughs were housing authorities[1] and exercised powers concurrently. Only the L.C.C. however had power to provide houses outside the county, a power which it had exercised to such effect that it owned at the time of the Herbert Commission about 94,000 such houses,[2] in addition to the 100,000 which it had built within the county.

Apart from this problem of what was to be done with the L.C.C. houses, there was also the question of whether some of the new London boroughs with particularly acute housing problems would be able to solve those problems in isolation. London's housing needs were unevenly distributed. Many of the inner boroughs (in the old L.C.C. area) were likely to find great difficulty both because of the sheer size of the areas needing redevelopment and replacement of obsolete housing, and because of the lack of sites for new housing and the high cost of developing those which could be found. Many of the outer boroughs, on the other hand, had neither the same need to provide houses nor the same acute shortage of sites.

These difficulties pointed to the need for some additional means of dealing with London housing apart from conferring basic powers on the boroughs. The White Paper had proposed[3] that the Greater London Council should have reserve housing powers within Greater London to be exercised with the consent of the borough concerned,

---

[1] This unique situation (no other county had concurrent powers) arose from the fact that the L.C.C. had inherited housing powers from the Metropolitan Board of Works at a time when the metropolitan boroughs did not exist.

[2] See Herbert *Report*, para. 362.

[3] *London Government* (Cmnd. 1562), paras. 28–30.

and should have sole powers for building outside Greater London; it was also proposed that the L.C.C.'s houses should be transferred to the G.L.C. for the time being but should ultimately come under local ownership and management.

Accordingly, the 1963 Act put the London boroughs and the City on a similar footing to county boroughs elsewhere with regard to most housing powers, but also gave the G.L.C. specific powers to build houses both inside and outside Greater London on the lines indicated in the White Paper.[1] It also provided that the G.L.C. should continue to have all the powers previously exercised by the L.C.C. 'until such date as the Minister may by order appoint'.[2] The Minister explained in the course of the proceedings on the Bill that this was intended simply as a transitional measure until the new boroughs were in a position to take on these powers.[3] It meant, for example, in relation to slum clearance, that the G.L.C. would only have powers in this transitional period and only in inner London, a fact which received a good deal of criticism from the Labour opposition in Parliament, who argued that the boroughs would not all be able to deal adequately with their slums unless they could call in the help of the G.L.C.[4]

The G.L.C. were given power to build within Greater London without the need to get the consent of the borough or boroughs concerned only if the housing was needed to rehouse people displaced by other activities of the G.L.C. (e.g. road building); or in an area of comprehensive development.[5] In other cases the consent of the borough was required although the G.L.C. could appeal to the Minister of Housing and Local Government if consent was refused.[6] The G.L.C. were also given power to take part in schemes under the Town Development Act, 1952, a power which elsewhere was exercised by county districts and county boroughs.[7] Under such schemes local authorities who were willing to help the more congested areas could agree to act jointly with the 'exporting' authority to provide housing and industrial sites on the basis of shared costs. The L.C.C. had made a number of such agreements with places like Haverhill in Suffolk and Basingstoke in Hampshire, as a further means of attempting to relieve London's housing problems by dispersal.

Two other provisions of the Act relating to housing are also worth

[1] 1963 Act, Section 21.
[2] ibid., Section 21(5).
[3] Standing Committee Proceedings, February 14, 1963, cols. 246–52.
[4] ibid., cols. 220–41; cf. Lords debates, May 20, 1963, cols. 23–52.
[5] See below, p. 55.
[6] 1963 Act, Section 21(4).
[7] ibid., Section 61.

noting. The G.L.C. was to maintain a record for Greater London of housing needs. How exactly this was to be done was left to the G.L.C. to decide, but it was certainly intended that the boroughs and the City were to act as agents in providing the necessary information to the G.L.C.; the information would be derived from housing applications many of which would in the normal way be made to the boroughs.[1] As an extension of this central agency function, the G.L.C. was also to provide an exchange service for people wanting to move either within Greater London or elsewhere; again, it was left to the G.L.C. to devise the means for doing this.[2]

The other important provision was that relating to the transfer of housing between the G.L.C. and the boroughs. The G.L.C. was to submit to the Minister within five years (i.e. by April 1, 1970) a programme for the transfer of housing accommodation owned by them to the boroughs. The Minister could in any case make an order for such transfer which might incidentally permit the G.L.C. to retain the right to nominate tenants to the transferred housing.[3]

In housing perhaps even more than in the case of traffic and highways, it will be seen that the Act laid down a unique division of functions between the G.L.C. and the boroughs. The boroughs were to be primary authorities within their own areas, but unlike county boroughs or even county districts elsewhere they had to have regard to the needs of the whole area of which they each formed a part, as represented by the specific powers and duties which were assigned to the G.L.C. The position was complicated by the transitional powers inherited by the G.L.C. from the L.C.C., and also by the uncertainty in the initial period after the new authorities were set up of how large would be the stock of housing retained by the G.L.C.

PLANNING

The Act's provisions with regard to planning are in many ways the most complicated in the whole Act, and a description of their main characteristics requires reference to certain important Regulations made under the Act. The basic position was stated to be that 'the Greater London Council shall be the local planning authority for Greater London as a whole', and 'the local planning authority as

[1] 1963 Act, Section 22 (1) to (4); applications were to be made to the boroughs by anyone living there, and to the G.L.C. by anyone else; in the case of borough applications the boroughs were to give information about the application to the G.L.C. including action taken by them to meet housing needs.

[2] ibid., Section 22(5).

[3] ibid., Section 23 (3) and (4); the provisions went wider than is indicated here but the G.L.C./borough transfers are the most important.

respects any London borough shall be the council of the borough and as respects the City shall be the Common Council'.[1] These provisions made it clear that neither the G.L.C. nor the boroughs was to have the exclusive right to settle London's planning, but the exact division of powers between them was a major source of the complexity of the provisions.

In the first place, it was made clear that applications for planning permission were to be made to the boroughs or the City, and decided by them, except that the Minister could prescribe that certain classes of planning application were to be decided instead by the G.L.C.[2] The definition of these classes was obviously of great importance to the relations between the G.L.C. and the boroughs and to the division of powers between them. It is not therefore surprising that there was a good deal of discussion between the Ministry of Housing and Local Government and the various affected parties, following the passing of the Act, on the exact scope of the Regulations. In the event it was decided that the G.L.C. should deal with the following:

(i) planning applications in certain specified areas of comprehensive development, mostly in eastern and south-eastern areas of London such as Stepney or Bermondsey, but also including the South Bank and Knightsbridge Green. These were all areas which had been proposed for comprehensive development by the L.C.C., largely because they were too big for the individual metropolitan boroughs' resources and which the G.L.C. therefore inherited.
(ii) applications for development which might have important consequences for the G.L.C.'s traffic responsibilities; these were defined specifically in five groups, e.g. 'the use of land as a ground for sports or games or as a racing track having, in any such case, the capacity to accommodate more than 2,500 spectators.'
(iii) applications to extract minerals on a large scale.[3]

But in addition to the applications which the boroughs had to pass to the G.L.C. for decision, the Act made provision, also by ministerial order, for certain classes of application to be referred to the G.L.C. by the boroughs before decision, the G.L.C. having the power to give directions on how they were to be dealt with.[4] This power was subject to definite limitations on the extent and manner of giving directions. Consequently, it was all the more difficult to devise

[1] 1963 Act, Section 24 (2) and (3).
[2] ibid., Section 24(4).
[3] The Town and Country Planning (Local Planning Authorities in Greater London) Regulations, 1965 (S.I. 1965 No. 679), Reg. 3.
[4] 1963 Act, Section 24(6).

precise Regulations which would be acceptable to both the G.L.C. and the boroughs, and the Regulations published in 1965[1] are not likely to be the last word on the subject. They deal with a variety of applications including large shops, tall buildings, certain industrial and office development, and development 'within 220 feet from the centre of a metropolitan road'; again showing a preoccupation with applications which could have repercussions on other responsibilities of the G.L.C. particularly in the traffic and highways fields, although the Regulations are not exclusively concerned with this.[2]

Further Regulations deal with the procedure to be followed where a borough wishes to approve an application which is not in conformity with the development plan, and with cases which must be referred to the Minister.[3] But perhaps even more difficult and controversial are the limitations on the G.L.C.'s power to give directions to the boroughs. They are only to have regard to certain matters in considering applications; for example, in relation to tall buildings, they are only to consider 'the suitability of the location for a building of the height proposed and the effect which the proposed building will have upon the skyline'.[4]

Consideration of planning applications is then one sphere in which the 1963 Act and Regulations made under it attempted to define the respective powers of the G.L.C. and the boroughs with no similar situation elsewhere in the country to give a guide. But the planning system depends on there being adequate plans setting out what kind of development the authority believes to be suitable to different parts of its area and what its general policy is. These 'development plans' are in the rest of the country produced by counties and county boroughs and subject to the approval of the Minister.[5] For London the 1963 Act did two things: it first provided that from April 1, 1965, the existing development plans relating to the area of Greater London[6] should together constitute the initial development plan for Greater London. This was no more than an interim measure designed to ensure continuity. Secondly, the Act attempted to define

---

[1] S.I. 1965 No. 679, Reg. 4.

[2] e.g., they also deal with applications involving the demolition of historic buildings.

[3] ibid., Regs. 5 and 6.

[4] ibid., Reg. 7(b).

[5] Under the Town and Country Planning Act, 1968, development plans are being replaced by structure plans, and local plans, though initially only in certain areas.

[6] i.e. the plans of the London and Middlesex C.C.s, Croydon, East Ham and West Ham C.B.s and parts of the plans of the Surrey, Essex, Kent and Hertfordshire C.C.s.

more precisely what was intended by making both the G.L.C. and the boroughs local planning authorities.

First, the G.L.C. was to conduct a survey of its area and make a report on this survey to the Minister, at the same time submitting a Greater London Development Plan (G.L.D.P.). This was to deal with general policy on the use of land in Greater London; significantly, the Act specifically referred to the fact that this should include 'guidance as to the future road system'.[1] The date of submission of this plan and the details of what it should contain were to be left to Regulations. It should be noted that this plan when approved by the Minister was not to supersede the initial plan, although it could amend it.

The final stage in the introduction of the new system was to be the preparation of the local or borough (including the City) plans. After the Greater London plan had been approved by the Minister the boroughs were to carry out surveys and prepare local development plans to be submitted to the G.L.C.; within the general framework of the G.L.D.P. these plans could add to or modify the existing provisions relating to the borough area, i.e. those in the initial development plan as modified by the G.L.D.P. These borough plans were to be submitted by the G.L.C. to the Minister with any observations they might have. The final stage would then end with the Minister's approval of the local plans when for the purposes of the Planning Acts the G.L.D.P. and the local plan together would constitute the development plan for each borough.[2]

Regulations, issued in 1966,[3] specified that the G.L.D.P. was to consist of a written statement, a map showing the main roads, and any other appropriate maps. The written statement was to include twenty different matters set out in the Regulations, among them statements of general policy on population, residential densities, and employment, and how these were likely to affect each London borough; statements of proposals on main roads and major traffic interchange points; statements of policy on the Green Belt and provision of public open spaces; and a statement indicating where major shopping centres were or should be. The form of the borough local development plans was to be similar, but the Regulations were less specific about the content of the written statements. They were,

[1] 1963 Act, Section 25(3).

[2] 1963 Act, Section 25 (4) and (5). Under Section 12 and the First Schedule of the Town and Country Planning Act, 1968, both the Greater London Development Plan and the borough plans will be structure plans, that is, statements of broad planning aims for each area.

[3] The Town and Country Planning (Development Plans for Greater London) Regulations, 1966 (S.I. 1966, No. 48).

however, to include a summary of the main proposals of the development plan; an indication of the period covered by the plan and the stages by which it was to be implemented; and a statement of the acreages and number of persons in primarily residential areas.

It will be seen that these are long-term provisions. The date of submission of the G.L.D.P. was fixed as the end of July 1969. A prolonged public enquiry will then be needed before the Minister will be in a position to approve it. After that will follow the borough plans. Clearly one sensitive point in these arrangements is the possibility that a borough might want to put something in its plan which conflicted with the G.L.C.'s policy. The Act laid down a procedure which effectively gave the Minister power to decide whether a particular proposal was in conformity with the G.L.D.P.[1]

Further specific provisions dealing with G.L.C./borough relations made the latter agents of the G.L.C. for the purposes of carrying out the Greater London surveys[2] and, most importantly, laid on the G.L.C. the obligation to consult the boroughs on their proposals for a G.L.D.P. and allow them an opportunity to make representations.[3] Correspondingly, the boroughs were to give the G.L.C. information when preparing their plans and to give them an opportunity to make representations.[4]

These then in essentials were the provisions designed to give both the G.L.C. and the boroughs a say in the planning of Greater London. Many incidental and consequential matters were also dealt with in the Act (e.g. the provision that lists of buildings of special architectural or historic interest should be kept both by the G.L.C. and the boroughs[5]) but for the most part these were designed to ensure that provisions of the Planning Acts could be applied to the unique situation created in London.

The three functions or rather groups of functions which have been considered above are all ones in which the London system differs markedly from that in the rest of the country and in which there is a major sharing of functions between the G.L.C. and the boroughs. The remaining functions of local authorities in Greater London as set out in the 1963 Act can be dealt with more briefly not because they are necessarily less important but because they do not have (or not to the same degree) these characteristics.

[1] 1963 Act, Section 27(1).
[2] ibid., Section 27(2)
[3] ibid., Section 27(3).
[4] ibid., Section 27(4).
[5] ibid., Section 28.

EDUCATION

So far as the twenty Outer London boroughs were concerned, i.e. those formed from areas formerly in Middlesex, Surrey, Essex, Kent and Hertfordshire, the Act's provisions were straightforward; they simply made these borough councils the local education authority.[1] The position in the old L.C.C. area was rather more complicated. The intention, as has been indicated, was to preserve intact the L.C.C. education service, but the question was how this was to be achieved. The solution put forward was for the G.L.C. to set up a special committee for this Inner London Education Area as it was to be known; the G.L.C. when acting through this committee as the local education authority for this area was to be known as the Inner London Education Authority (I.L.E.A.).[2] Both the composition of this special committee and its relationship to the G.L.C. are unusual.

The I.L.E.A. was to consist, first, of all the G.L.C. councillors elected for the inner London boroughs and the City, and, secondly, of one member each chosen by each of the boroughs and the City.[3] No other education authority in England and Wales has its composition prescribed by statute for the simple reason that the authority is usually identical with the county or county borough council. The reason for not making the G.L.C. itself the L.E.A. is twofold; first, the G.L.C. area was not identical with that of the education area for which it was to be responsible; secondly, the Government had gone on record in the White Paper on London Government as desiring to give the inner boroughs some voice in education, and this was to be achieved by the device of having indirect borough representation. It should also be noted that the I.L.E.A., like any other education authority, has to appoint an education committee whose membership must include people 'of experience in education' and 'acquainted with the educational conditions prevailing in the area'.[4]

It was made clear in the Act that the I.L.E.A. was to be practically autonomous in financial matters, determining the amount for which the G.L.C. was to precept on the inner boroughs for education purposes, and also the amounts needed for capital expenditure. It was also to appoint the necessary staff, including most importantly a chief education officer.[5] In these respects the I.L.E.A. was analogous

[1] 1963 Act, Section 30(1) (a).
[2] ibid., Section 30(1) (b).
[3] ibid., Section 30(2).
[4] See Education Act, 1944, First Schedule, Part II.
[5] 1963 Act, Section 30 (3) and (4).

to the police or watch committee of a local authority which also determines necessary expenditure, and appoints a chief constable without having to go through the normal procedures of the authority.[1]

There was one other point of considerable interest in the Act's provisions relating to the I.L.E.A. This was the duty laid on the Minister of Education (now the Secretary for Education and Science) to review and report on by March 31, 1970, the administration of education in inner London 'for the purpose of determining whether, and if so to what extent, in what part or parts of that Area, and subject to what, if any conditions all or any of the functions of the local education authority relating to education should be transferred to, or to a body including a member or members appointed by, the appropriate council',[2] i.e. of an inner borough or the City. These words caused much debate during the passage of the Bill, members of the Labour Opposition claiming that the object was to achieve a break-up of the I.L.E.A. and to transfer education to the boroughs as in outer London, although this was denied by Sir Edward Boyle, the Minister of Education who said that the review would be a completely open one.[3] In the event, however, the Labour Government which succeeded the Conservatives in 1964 determined to make the I.L.E.A. permanent and these provisions relating to a review were therefore repealed.[4]

Some other points relating to education may also be noted. One of the main reasons for retaining the L.C.C. area for education was that it had long been planned as a unit without regard to the boundaries of the boroughs within it. Fears were expressed that there would be difficulties in outer London if boroughs adhered too rigidly to the idea of making themselves completely independent units. The Act expressly laid a duty on the outer boroughs to consult with neighbouring authorities before revising their education plans in order to make sure that they had adequately provided for the movement of schoolchildren across borough boundaries; and authorities were forbidden to make it a ground for excluding children from their schools that they lived in another authority's area either elsewhere in Greater London or adjoining it.[5]

There were finally a number of provisions designed to make the transition between the old and the new systems in Greater London.

[1] Police Act 1964, Section 2.
[2] 1963 Act, Section 30(6).
[3] H.C. Deb., Vol. 669, cols. 246–8, December 11, 1962.
[4] Local Government (Termination of Reviews) Act, 1967, Section 2.
[5] 1963 Act, Section 31(8).

One subject which was to cause difficulty was the provision of a school health service in inner London, since as a result of the re-organisation proposals there were now to be different authorities responsible for the education and the health services in this area, the latter being assigned to the boroughs. The Act proposed that the I.L.E.A. and the boroughs should prepare a joint scheme to deal with two matters: (i) the joint use of professional staff, premises and equipment for the school health service and the general health services; (ii) consultation about the qualifications, etc., of professional staff to be appointed to these services.[1] These schemes were to be jointly approved by the Ministers of Education and Health.

ENVIRONMENTAL HEALTH SERVICES

This term covers a whole group of services coming under the Public Health Acts, including sewerage, refuse collection and disposal, parks and the sanitary functions performed by public health inspectors. In general, the London Government Act made the boroughs the authorities for these functions,[2] but with some important exceptions which are noted below. These exceptions relate primarily to the sewerage and refuse disposal functions.

Sewerage and sewage disposal. The provisions of the London Government Act are best understood by reference to the pre-existing situation. In general, sewerage authorities are county borough and county district authorities, but this is a field where for technical efficiency some authorities combine in joint boards to carry our their duties. In the case of the counties of London and Middlesex before 1965, however, the situation was unique in that both the county councils were responsible for main sewerage[3] in their areas with the district councils having responsibility for local sewers. The sewerage areas in fact extended beyond the county boundaries, the L.C.C. including for example West Ham and Willesden, and Middlesex C.C. Barnet and Chingford. The London Government Act applied this situation to most of Greater London by creating a sewerage area of the Greater London Council within which the G.L.C. was to be responsible for main sewers and sewage disposal, and the boroughs for other public sewers.[4] It should be noted that because this area was constituted from the areas of existing sewage authorities it did not take

[1] ibid., Section 32.

[2] ibid., Section 40(2).

[3] That is for sewers which were mainly designed to carry sewage away from the local sewers to which most premises are directly connected (see 1963 Act, Section 39(1) (a)).

[4] 1963 Act, Section 35 (1) to (3).

in the whole of Greater London but did take in some areas which were outside Greater London.[1] The Act provided that, in those areas of Greater London not within the G.L.C. sewerage area, the boroughs should be responsible for all sewers. Even this was, however, subject to an important exception in that most of the London boroughs of Bexley and Bromley were covered by the West Kent Main Sewerage Board which was to continue to perform its functions.[2] Thus the position of the G.L.C. remained somewhat anomalous and it was therefore provided that that authority should review the position immediately after April 1, 1965, and make proposals for the transfer to them of any sewers or works in Greater London which they considered should form part of the main system. These proposals which were to operate not later than April 1, 1970, were to follow the normal procedure of enquiries under the Public Health Acts. After 1970 the G.L.C. were to have a general duty to keep the situation under review.[3]

Refuse collection and disposal. Here again the Act imposed a division of functions which was not to be found anywhere else in the country. Elsewhere, county boroughs and county districts are responsible for both collection and disposal. In London, the G.L.C. was made responsible for disposal and the boroughs for collection, on the grounds argued by the Herbert Commission that whereas collection was a local function, disposal in a large metropolitan area posed such formidable problems that it needed to be organised over the area as a whole.[4]

Parks. Provision of parks and open spaces has been historically a public health function, although now more naturally thought of as an amenity-provision. In Greater London before 1965 parks were generally provided by the county boroughs and county districts, although the London County Council was active in this field being responsible for such extensive open spaces as Hampstead Heath. The 1963 Act made both the G.L.C. and the boroughs authorities for the purpose of the provision of parks.[5] The provisions relating to the G.L.C. were, however, subject to two important qualifications. First, they were to take over the parks and open spaces of the London and Middlesex county councils, but by 1975 at the latest they had to submit a scheme to the Minister indicating which areas of land they proposed to retain and why, and proposing the transfer of the re-

[1] See map, p. 190.
[2] 1963 Act, Section 35 (4) and (9).
[3] ibid., Section 35 (5) and (6).
[4] Cmnd. 1164, paras. 635–58: 1963 Act, Sch. 11.
[5] 1963 Act, Section 58(1).

mainder to the borough or boroughs within whose area they were situated. Secondly, they could provide further parks for the most part only if they were 'approved by the Minister as being for the benefit of an area of Greater London substantially larger than the London boroughs in or near which the park or open space is proposed to be provided'.[1] Thus in intention it appeared that the G.L.C. were to be the providers of what might be called London parks and the boroughs of local parks.

Control of building. A small but important part of the Public Health Acts was concerned with the administration and enforcement of standards relating to the construction of buildings. Outside the county of London there was a uniform system administered by county boroughs and county districts. Within the county of London the situation was much more complicated, and the position was governed by a special series of London Building Acts.[2] The 1963 London Government Act went some way towards assimilating the unique London system to that operating elsewhere, and eliminated some of the London Building Acts' provisions which were no longer required since they were covered by other legislation. But a number of these provisions were retained with the substitution of the G.L.C. for the L.C.C., the effect being to make the G.L.C. the responsible authority in Inner London (including the City) for matters relating to the structural stability, etc., of buildings whereas in Outer London these matters were dealt with by the London boroughs under general Regulations of the Ministry of Housing and Local Government.[3]

Port health authority. One other point may be mentioned about the environmental health provisions in the 1963 Act. The City of London was to be the port health authority for the Port of London, with duties extending from Teddington Lock, almost on the boundary of Greater London, to the mouth of the Thames. This was in fact no different from the existing system, but it draws attention to a minor but remarkable feature of London's government, the special relationship of the City to the port which now extends well beyond the boundaries of the City, especially in the direction of Tilbury where there is now a major concentration of docks. However, the main responsibility for London's port rests with the Port of London Authority.

The sections of the Act relating to the public health provisions are

[1] ibid., Section 58 (1) and (2).

[2] An account will be found in the Herbert *Report*, paras, 881–8.

[3] 1963 Act, Section 43: the Minister did however hold out the hope that ultimately it might be possible to assimilate the London provisions completely to those in the rest of the country (London Government Bill, Proceedings of Standing Committee F, twelfth sitting, March 5, 1963, col. 598).

among the most complicated in the whole Act. This is not as in the case of planning because of the complexity of the provisions themselves. It is rather because for historical reasons a somewhat different system had grown up in the County of London – the main public Health Act of 1936 was paralleled by the Public Health (London) Act 1936 – and the 1963 Act attempted to assimilate most of these provisions. There remain, however, some anomalies parallel with those relating to building control mentioned above.[1]

OTHER PROVISIONS

Personal health, welfare and children's services. As with the environmental health services, the boroughs (and the City) were to be the authorities responsible for these services, except that the G.L.C. was to take responsibility for the ambulance service.[2] Indeed these services constituted, together with education in the outer boroughs, the most important group of functions for which the boroughs had exclusive powers. They thus in this case were to have the same powers as county boroughs elsewhere. This represented a fundamental change in the London situation, where until 1965, all these services were provided by the county councils and the three county boroughs of Croydon, East Ham and West Ham. It was also a quite different situation from that in the environmental health services, many of which before 1965 were provided by the county districts. That it was reasonable to make an exception of the ambulance service and organise it on a Greater London basis was generally accepted.[3] But attempts were made during the passage of the Bill to get an Inner London Children Authority established on the lines of the I.L.E.A., largely on the grounds that it would be wrong to break up a service which was being well run by the L.C.C. This attempt failed; to have conceded it would have been an admission by the Government that it was not possible to make the boroughs the primary units of local government, as had all along been the avowed aim.

One other small point is of interest here. The Act gave the G.L.C. the power together with the boroughs to make contributions to voluntary organisations operating in these social service fields.[4]

---

[1] e.g. the G.L.C. was to retain powers inherited from the L.C.C. to make bye-laws dealing with such things as demolition of buildings, sanitary conveniences and refuse incinerators in *inner London only*. (Schedule 11, Pt. II, paras. 2–4).

[2] 1963 Act, Sections 45 (1) and (3); 46(1); 47(1).

[3] As had been recommended by the Herbert Commission.

[4] 1963 Act, Sections 45(4); 46(3); 47(4).

This was a recognition of the fact that in London these organisations did not necessarily confine their activities to the area of a single borough.

Fire service. This was to be a function of the G.L.C.[1] who would thus take over the whole of the brigades maintained by the county councils of London and Middlesex and by the three county boroughs as well as parts of the brigades of the other counties. Again, there was little dispute that if there was to be a G.L.C. it was right that it should be responsible for the fire service.

Libraries were to be the responsibility of the boroughs, a natural development since the metropolitan boroughs and a majority of the county districts in the area were already library authorities.[2]

Civil defence. In civil defence there was to be a split in functions between the G.L.C. and the boroughs corresponding to that between county councils and district councils elsewhere in the country.[3]

For most remaining local authority functions the London boroughs were to be the responsible authority. These included a wide variety of *regulatory and licensing* functions such as those under the Food and Drugs Act,[4] the Offices, Shops and Railway Premises Act,[5] the Riding Establishments Act[6] and the Fireworks Act.[7] Some powers were, however, reserved to the G.L.C These were mostly powers which had been possessed by the L.C.C. and were extended to Greater London mainly because it was felt that there were special circumstances relating to London; elsewhere county borough councils mainly exercise these functions. They include the licensing of theatres and other places of public entertainment,[8] the licensing of greyhound racing tracks for betting,[9] and the issue of licences to premises used for storing petrol.[10]

There were in addition a number of other miscellaneous functions which were to be exercised by the G.L.C., including the provision of smallholdings, elsewhere a county council function.[11] The G.L.C. as well as the boroughs were to be authorised to provide entertainments, and in this connection the G.L.C. were to inherit from the L.C.C.

[1] ibid., Section 48.
[2] 1963 Act, Section 56.
[3] ibid., Section 49; these provisions have been superseded by the Government's decision in 1968 to run down the civil defence organisation.
[4] ibid., Section 54.
[5] ibid., Section 51.
[6] ibid., Section 62(1).
[7] ibid., Section 50(1).
[8] ibid., Section 52.
[9] ibid., Section 53.
[10] ibid., Section 50(2).
[11] ibid., Section 55.

E

certain important properties including the Royal Festival Hall, the Crystal Palace and Kenwood.[1]

Finally, it may be noted that another unique arrangement was devised for land drainage and flood prevention. In most of the rest of the country these functions are the responsibility of river authorities, at least as regards the major aspects. Under the 1963 Act the G.L.C. was to be the land drainage authority for an area of 400 square miles including most of the old L.C.C. area, west Middlesex and parts of Kent and Surrey. For the main rivers in this area the G.L.C. was to be the sole authority responsible for flood prevention, etc., but for the lesser rivers responsibility was to be shared with the boroughs.[2]

Apart from the constitution of the new authorities and distribution of functions between them, the 1963 Act dealt with a number of other matters, of which the most important was the question of *finance*. The boroughs were to be rating authorities and to be eligible for general and rate-deficiency grants.[3] Consequently, the G.L.C. was to precept on the boroughs for the amounts required from the rates for G.L.C. services. Because different services covered different areas, the G.L.C. precept could not be uniform for all the boroughs. Thus the inner boroughs, i.e. those formed out of the metropolitan boroughs, would have to raise money for education as a G.L.C. service. Again, those boroughs which came into the G.L.C.'s sewerage area or the land drainage area would have to meet precepts for these purposes.

An important provision gave the Minister power to make a rate equalisation scheme.[4] The object was to try to ensure less disparity in the rates to be levied by the different London boroughs. It was obvious for example that the borough to be formed from Bethnal Green, Poplar and Stepney would have greater problems and less resources to meet them than the borough which was to consist of Paddington, St Marylebone and Westminster. A rate equalisation scheme had been in operation in the L.C.C. area and under it the richer metropolitan boroughs made a contribution to the poorer boroughs. The Act now made it possible for such a scheme to be introduced for the whole of Greater London.

There were finally some temporary provisions in the Act for meeting the unusual situation during the change-over from the old to the new system. Provision was made for example to cover the expenses of the new authorities during the year 1964–5 when they would

---

[1] ibid., Section 57.
[2] ibid., Sch. 14.
[3] ibid., Sections 63–5.
[4] ibid., Section 66.

exist side by side with the old.[1] More interesting was the provision under which the G.L.C. was to meet part of the additional expenditure, if any, incurred by the counties which were to lose territory to Greater London (Essex, Hertfordshire, Kent and Surrey). Where the county's additional rate burden exceeded the product of a fivepenny rate, the G.L.C. was to pay on a tapering scale beginning with the whole amount of the excess in 1965–6 and diminishing to one-eighth of the excess in 1972–3 by yearly stages.[2] This provision was the subject of some debate during the proceedings on the Bill, the original clause having been less generous to the counties. The Government were pressed among other things to make the excess costs of the reorganisation a charge on the Exchequer on the grounds that 'the whole situation is created by the Government as a matter of national policy'.[3] To this the Government spokesman replied that 'This is essentially a local government expense. . . . It is something that is inherent in all local government reorganisation.'[4] There was some truth in both remarks. The Government's view was in keeping with the traditional approach to changes in local government boundaries and functions; for example, county borough extensions which frequently involved counties in financial loss, had always been dealt with by means of financial adjustments between the authorities concerned.[5] On the other hand, the scale of the London reorganisation far exceeded anything previously attempted since the late nineteenth century, and represented the Government's attempt to deal with a situation which the local authorities themselves did not generally want to see changed. Nevertheless, they were probably right to treat it as basically a local government matter, although one of an unusual nature.

The unusual nature of the operation was also emphasised by the Act's provisions with regard to staffing, and in particular the requirement that the Minister was to establish a staff commission with the general duty of keeping under review the staffing arrangements for the new authorities, and advising the Minister on problems arising in the transitional period particularly in relation to safeguarding the interests of the staff affected.[6]

Staff matters had figured prominently in the discussions and negotiations which preceded the introduction of the London Government

[1] ibid., Section 69.
[2] ibid., Section 70.
[3] Mr Michael Stewart, Standing Committee F, London Government Bill, 17th Day (March 14, 1963), col. 839.
[4] ibid., col. 856 (Mr F. V. Corfield, Parly. Sec. Miny. of Housing and L. Govt.).
[5] See Local Government Act, 1933, Section 151.
[6] 1963 Act, Section 85(5).

Bill into Parliament. The natural anxieties of the staff who were going
to be affected by the reorganisation were effectively brought to the
attention of the Government, particularly by the L.C.C. Staff
Association, whose membership, being confined to the L.C.C.,
naturally had the closest interest in the reorganisation. It was the
L.C.C. Staff Association which first put forward the idea of an independent body to oversee the staffing arrangements in the interim
period when the new authorities were being set up, and this idea
emerged as the staff commission under the Act.

Although it was only a temporary body,[1] the interest of the staff
commission lies in the possibility that it may serve as a precedent
for similar arrangements if widespread changes are made in local
government structure and functions following the report of the Royal
Commission on Local Government in England.

It is also worth noting that apart from the appointment of a staff
commission, the Act provided other safeguards for staff, notably by
laying down that anyone transferred to 'duties reasonably comparable
to those in which he was engaged immediately before the date of
transfer'[2] should have at least as favourable a salary scale and terms
of employment as he had before.

Of the remaining provisions of the Act, mostly of a minor or consequential nature, only three need be mentioned. First, there was a
requirement that the boroughs should appoint an architect. This was
rather an odd provision for several reasons. It was not in the Bill
as originally presented but inserted at the Committee stage on the
motion of the Minister, Sir Keith Joseph; and it conflicted with the
idea that local authorities should by and large appoint chief officers
as they think fit.[3] Furthermore, it inevitably led to demands that the
Act should specify other chief officers whom it was desirable that
boroughs should appoint, e.g. housing managers.[4] The Minister
himself conceded that he was standing on a 'slippery slope' in
moving the amendment, but justified it, not altogether convincingly,
on the grounds that the boroughs were taking on new and important
responsibilities in the planning field which made it imperative that
they should have separate architect's departments specified in the Act.

Secondly, the Act required the G.L.C. to establish 'an organisation
for the purpose of conducting, or assisting in the conducting of,
investigations into, and the collecting of information relating to,

[1] It began work in April 1963 and ceased in December 1965 (See *Report* of
London Government Staff Commission, H.M.S.O., 1966).

[2] 1963 Act, Section 85(3).

[3] Except for the 'traditional' appointments of Clerk, Treasurer, etc. (Local
Government Act, 1933, Sections 98–107).

[4] Standing Committee F, 19th Sitting (March 19, 1963), cols. 925–30.

any matters concerning Greater London or any part thereof', and making the results available not only to local authorities but to central departments and the public.[1]

The cumbersome legal language concealed a development which was potentially of great importance, the establishment of a centre for research and intelligence within the G.L.C. but serving wider needs than simply the administrative needs of that body. The idea of an Intelligence Department as part of the G.L.C.'s administration had been strongly argued by the Herbert Commission,[2] and the Act gave the G.L.C. wide discretion in the scope of this new organisation. This unique statutory provision emphasised, however, the difference between London's local government and that of other large cities and conurbations. County boroughs could undertake their own statistical and other enquiries for their own areas, but there was no machinery except voluntary arrangements with their neighbours for instituting enquiries over a wider area such as a conurbation.

The third miscellaneous provision of the Act which is of interest was one giving power to the G.L.C. specifically to publicise the amenities and advantages of Greater London other than commercial and industrial advantages.[3] The object was primarily to meet frequently heard criticisms of local authorities that they did not do enough to keep members of the public informed about their activities, but the Act's provisions went wider than, although obviously including, giving information about local authority services.[4]

As has been suggested, the London Government Act of 1963 is a formidable document, and only became law after a prolonged political struggle. It constituted the framework within which the G.L.C. and the London boroughs have had to operate a distinctive new system of local government since April 1, 1965. In the following chapters we consider the nature of these new authorities, and the way in which they have tackled some of the problems and difficulties confronting them.

[1] 1963 Act, Section 71.
[2] See above, p. 40.
[3] 1963 Act, Section 73.
[4] The restriction on publicising commercial, etc., advantages was to avoid conflict with Government policies on location of employment.

Chapter IV

THE NEW AUTHORITIES

A. ADMINISTRATIVE ARRANGEMENTS

Problems of transfer of functions

The reorganisation of local government which took place in Greater London following the 1963 Act was on a scale unprecedented since the local government system had been established in the late nineteenth century. If the Radcliffe-Maud Commission's proposals[1] are implemented the remainder of the country will be faced with a huge task of reorganisation. It is not without interest, therefore, to see how the new authorities came into being and how the voters reacted to them.

During the comparatively short period between the election of the new authorities in the spring of 1964 and their assumption of their new responsibilities on April 1, 1965, they had much to do in the way of recruiting staff, settling departmental and committee structures and arranging the transfer of functions. At the same time, the old authorities remained in being with full responsibility for carrying on services until March 31, 1965. The simultaneous disappearance on April 1, 1965, of all existing authorities, with the exception of the City of London and Harrow, together with the complete redistribution of functions provided the main difficulties of the transitional period.

The 1963 Act[2] made provision for the setting up of joint committees of existing authorities to make plans for the change-over. The G.L.C. Joint Committee had members from the London, Middlesex, Essex, Kent and Surrey County Councils, and the Croydon, East Ham and West Ham County Borough Councils; the London Borough Joint Committees from their constituent authorities. Some farsighted authorities established joint committees before the Act was passed and were thus able to make swifter progress.

Among the immediate issues facing the borough joint committees

---

[1] *Report* of Royal Commission on Local Government in England, 1966–1969 (Cmnd. 4040, H.M.S.O., June, 1969).
[2] Section 86.

was that of warding, a necessary preliminary to the holding of elections, and the provision of names for the new boroughs. Both these questions provoked a good deal of disagreement in a number of cases, and on the question of names some rather curious compromises were arrived at, such as Havering for the union of Romford and Hornchurch, and Hillingdon for Uxbridge, Ruislip-Northwood, Yiewsley & West Drayton and Hayes & Harlington. Often these were determined by the Minister of Housing and Local Government in default of agreement among the authorities themselves. Only in one case, the Royal Borough of Kensington and Chelsea, was the Minister defeated in his attempts to keep names simple and to avoid composite names.[1]

Both these questions illustrate a fundamental point about the borough joint committees. They had no power to commit the individual constituent authorities, or the new borough councils which were to succeed them, but only to recommend. Where there was disagreement on the joint committees, or where the committee agreed on a course of action but the constituent authorities did not accept their recommendations, the matter had to be left open until the new borough council had been elected. Nevertheless even in these cases the committees did a lot of useful preliminary work, e.g. in assembling information; and where there was close agreement among the constituent authorities a great many measures such as the standardisation of accounting procedures could be taken to ease the task facing the new boroughs.

Probably the most difficult questions for the G.L.C. and the boroughs concerned staffing and the transfer of functions. Not all functions provided the same difficulties. Where, as in the case of libraries or refuse collection, the problem was to assimilate the services carried on by each of the constituent authorities of a new borough, it was relatively easy. Much the most difficult problems arose over the transfer of county services to the boroughs, especially the children's and personal health and welfare services. Particular problems arose because buildings such as children's and old people's homes had been provided with county needs in mind and were not necessarily sited conveniently to serve the needs of the new boroughs. A simple division of existing homes among the boroughs in which they happened to be situated would have resulted in considerable over-provision in some boroughs and considerable under-provision in others.

This problem was one which the central departments (Home Office and Ministry of Health), the counties, the borough joint

[1] See Appendix, p. 187, for a list of the London boroughs.

committees and, from May 1964, the new boroughs wrestled with
over a considerable period of time beginning in some cases well
before the London Government Bill had completed its passage
through Parliament. The main difficulty was how to reconcile the
need to ensure that each borough received a fair allocation in relation to its needs with administrative arrangements which did not
become excessively complicated. But in the case of the 'severed'
counties of Essex, Kent and Surrey, there was the further difficulty
that a fair balance had to be struck between the needs of the new
boroughs and those of the counties which were to continue in being
although with reduced areas and populations.

The most important role in devising allocations of accommodation
was played by the counties, since they had the detailed knowledge
and experience of the services to be transferred. The central
departments were mainly concerned to ensure that generally
acceptable principles were established, although they had in
addition a much wider role especially in giving general advice and
guidance to the new authorities on their responsibilities. For the
joint committees and the new boroughs the main concern was fair
treatment.

To the outside observer the main impression is that these transfer
arrangements worked remarkably smoothly considering the difficulties. This is a tribute largely to the officers and members of
authorities who devoted much time and effort to them in addition
to carrying out their normal duties. That the machinery for considering these questions also proved to be somewhat complicated in
many cases is not surprising. This can be illustrated from what
happened in the L.C.C. area.

The wide spread of residential accommodation without regard
to the boundaries of the new London boroughs was particularly
evident in the L.C.C.'s provision of children's and old people's
homes. In recognition of the difficulties which would arise in making
provision for the transferred services, the Metropolitan Boroughs'
Standing Joint Committee[1] and the L.C.C. opened discussions in the
early part of 1963, that is, at a time when the London Government Bill
was still in progress in Parliament. The result of these discussions was a
memorandum dealing with proposals for the transfer of the children's
personal-health and welfare services, which was put to the borough joint

[1] The M.B.S.J.C. was established in 1912 to provide a means of discussing
matters of mutual interest and concern to the Metropolitan boroughs, and also
to represent them collectively in negotiations, e.g. with the L.C.C. and the government departments. A similar function is performed for the London boroughs
by the London Boroughs Association (see below, p. 83).

committees by the Metropolitan Boroughs' S.J.C. in November 1963.

More detailed proposals were then prepared by three working parties of L.C.C. and metropolitan borough officers, one for each of these services. They were set up at the end of 1963 and continued work until March 1965. These working parties went into great detail in specifying the arrangements for transfer; in addition they produced a number of more general memoranda about the problems and policies for the guidance of the boroughs. Their very considerable efforts proved essential for enabling the boroughs to take over services on April 1, 1965.

Allocation of residential accommodation and staffing were the two main problems dealt with by the working parties. An example of the former was children's homes. The working party on the children's service came to the conclusion that the fairest method was to allocate homes on the basis of estimated need for places for each borough. A borough which did not have homes with sufficient places situated within its own area would thus be allocated homes situated in other boroughs. Conversely, a borough within whose boundaries were homes providing more places than it was estimated to require would not inherit all of them. An exception to this rule was made in the case of certain large or specialised homes which would serve the needs of more than one borough. Here it was proposed to allocate a specific number of places to each of the two or more boroughs with a need for them, the control of the home being assigned to the borough taking most places. 'Joint-user' arrangements of this kind are a familiar feature in local government, most notably where accommodation is shared between hospital authorities (N.H.S.) and welfare authorities (counties and county boroughs).

The differing circumstances in the different counties which were to be merged either in whole or in part into Greater London were reflected in the arrangements for transfer of functions. In Surrey, for example, proposals were drawn up by the county council and readily accepted by the borough joint committees, reflecting the close and harmonious relations between the county council and the districts which the Herbert Commission had commented on.[1] A particular problem facing Surrey and the other 'severed' counties was to determine on what principles responsibility for people in homes on April 1, 1965, was to be assumed by either the county council or a London borough.[2] In general, the solution adopted was

[1] *Report* (Cmnd. 1164), para. 679.

[2] This situation arose, for example, where a children's home within the county but outside Greater London was to be retained by the county but contained children who had come from areas now to be included in Greater London.

for the authority from whose area the person had originally come to accept responsibility.

The London Government Staff Commission

One of the most urgent questions which had to be settled before April 1, 1965, was the staffing of the new authorities. Departmental complements had to be determined, the principles on which staff were to be transferred and recruited had to be decided and appointments had to be made in time for the new authorities to be fully operative on the appointed day. Some of these matters were in the hands of the joint committees and later, in 1964–5, of the new authorities. But the unusual nature of the whole operation was emphasised by the part played by the London Government Staff Commission, a statutory body with unique powers and duties.[1]

The Staff Commission's main job was to supervise the arrangements for recruitment and transfer of staff, and generally to safeguard the interests of the staff. It was a difficult assignment: on the one hand the staff already employed by authorities in Greater London were naturally anxious about the effects of the reorganisation on their position and careers; on the other, the new authorities wanted as much freedom as possible to recruit staff. Thus difficult questions arose: whether, for example, authorities should be able to advertise for staff on a national scale or whether they should confine their recruitment to staff already serving in Greater London.

It must be remembered that these questions arose only for a minority of the staff involved in the reorganisation. For the great majority, clerks and typists, dustmen and building workers, caretakers and groundsmen, reorganisation meant simply in the first place working for an authority with a different name—Camden instead of St Pancras, Redbridge instead of Ilford. The minority was, nevertheless, an important one, and included many senior officers, some professional and technical staff, and, generally, staff transferred from the counties, such as child care officers. For these officers, the main question was whether and, if so, where there would be a place for them in the new authorities.

In this situation, the Staff Commission were on the whole successful in meeting the fears of the staff without encroaching unduly on the authorities' cherished prerogative of choosing their own staff. In doing so they were helped by the fact that it became increasingly evident that there would be very little redundancy among existing

[1] See above, p. 67. The Chairman was Sir Harold Emmerson, a former Permanent Secretary of the Ministry of Labour; the other members were Lord Hemingford and Lord Geddes of Epsom.

staff. Of about 50,000 staff directly affected by the reorganisation, only 172 were declared redundant; more than half of these were over 60 and therefore close to retirement.[1]

The Staff Commission's own activities helped to reduce the risk of redundancy but another factor was the acute shortage of many professional and technical staff, such as architects, planners, and public health inspectors. For most chief officer posts the Commission persuaded the new authorities to give preference to candidates from the authority's own area; if no suitable candidate was found by this means they could widen the search to the remainder of Greater London. Only if the authority was still unable to find a satisfactory candidate could it then approach the Commission with a request to advertise the post nationally.

By these means, the great majority of posts in the new authorities were filled by staff of existing authorities. But although redundancy was not a major problem, there were many other problems. The question of status, for example, was bound to arise where, as with borough clerks' or treasurers' departments, there were to be fewer departments under the new system as compared with the old. Some felt aggrieved at the prospect of being fourth or fifth in the departmental hierarchy of a new borough whereas previously they had been nearer the top post, even though, as sometimes happened, their new posts were to be better paid than the old. Then there was the problem of transfers. Some officers felt that they had been unfairly treated under the arrangements for transfer to the new authorities. These and similar problems the Staff Commission helped to overcome, above all by establishing close relations with the staff associations and the authorities so that difficulties could be dealt with as they arose.

It can undoubtedly be said that the London Government Staff Commission fulfilled the main aim set for it by the Government, that of ensuring that staff interests were safeguarded. The National and Local Government Officer's Association have acknowledged this by making it an item of their policy to press for the establishment of similar bodies in any future reorganisation of local government. It is a more difficult question to decide how far this was achieved at the cost of making the new system more expensive or less efficient that it might otherwise have been.

The priorities as the Government saw them seem to have been: first, to reorganise the system of local government in Greater London to make it better fitted to undertake the tasks which needed

[1] *Report* of the London Government Staff Commission (H.M.S.O., 1966), para. 182.

doing; secondly, to ensure that the reorganisation was carried through smoothly. In this latter aim, the staff had a key role. The Government's fear of a breakdown in services was a major factor in their giving priority to the safeguarding of staff interests. It is certainly open to question whether the reorganisation could have been carried through so smoothly and successfully without the Staff Commission. A great deal of the preparatory work for the introduction of the new system fell on the staff of the existing authorities, and without their willing co-operation there might well have been chaos.

But could the reorganisation have been carried out with less strain? The size of the task was due mainly to the fact that there was a simultaneous redistribution of areas and functions. On the face of it, it might seem to be easier to carry out reorganisation in two stages. One possibility would be to amalgamate areas first and create new authorities which would be responsible for the functions of the authorities which they replace. At a later stage, there would be a re-distribution of functions. Another possibility in the London context might have been to have set up the London boroughs first with their new functions and then to have set up the G.L.C. at a later stage. Two-stage reorganisations of this kind carry the danger of prolonging the period of uncertainty and confusion.

Whatever method is adopted, a balance has to be struck. On the one hand, there are advantages in going ahead as quickly as possible once a decision has been taken to carry out reorganisation. On the other, there is a risk of confusion, if not breakdown, if the pressure is too great. A prolonged change-over may be unsettling; a short change-over may give insufficient time. In the London situation there were also political reasons for making the transitional period as short as possible.[1] Probably some lengthening of the period would have been desirable, but, as suggested above, the room for manoeuvre is small. Certainly in any future reorganisation of local government it is a question which merits close attention.

Constitution of the new authorities

The new authorities which came into being in Greater London in 1964 and assumed their responsibilities in 1965 constituted a new type of two-tier structure in local government in this country. It is therefore of some interest to see how these authorities have organised themselves for dealing with this situation, both internally, in

---

[1] The Government was anxious that the new authorities should be elected and arrangements for the reorganisation well advanced by the time of the General Election which could not be later than October 1964.

their committee and departmental structure, and externally, particularly in the co-operative machinery between the boroughs. But first we must note the unique constitution and powers of that survival from an earlier age, the Corporation of the City of London.

The Corporation of London. As was noted earlier, the London Government Act of 1963 made no changes in either the constitution or the powers of the City except to confer on it the additional powers of a London borough. Thus, for example, the City is now a children's authority in its own right, although in practice it has made an arrangement with the neighbouring London borough of Tower Hamlets whereby the latter provides a child-care service on an agency basis.

For the purposes of this account, three features of the City's position need to be mentioned. The first is that its constitution is unique among present-day local authorities, retaining some features deriving from a much earlier date, such as the Court of Aldermen.[1] For practical purposes of local government the City is governed by the Court of Common Council which consists of the Lord Mayor, twenty-five aldermen and 159 common councilmen, the latter corresponding to councillors in the London boroughs.[2] It is thus a very large council by present-day standards, particularly in relation to the size of the electorate. On the other hand, the City is wealthy to a degree which reflects its financial and commercial position: it has a rateable value of over £44 million, greater than that of Sheffield and Leeds combined, despite its resident population of only 4,200.[3]

The second point to note about the City is that its activities are not limited by the need to raise money on the rates. Alone among present-day local authorities, it derives income from corporate property which it is free to spend on activities which elsewhere would fall on the rates. This City's Cash, as it is called, thus enables the Corporation to undertake a wider range of functions than those which are conferred by statute. At the same time the City has, like other authorities, a rate fund for financing these latter functions.

Finally, the range of functions carried out by the City Corporation

[1] For the City's constitution, see the 'Statement made to the Royal Commission on Local Government in Greater London' (*Written Evidence*, Vol. 1, H.M.S.O., 1962, pp. 33–48); also, *The Corporation of London* (Oxford University Press, 1950).

[2] There are some differences, however; for example, candidates for Common Council must be freemen of the City.

[3] It must be remembered that about 375,000 people come daily into the City to work, giving it a daytime population higher than that of practically any of the London boroughs.

may be divided into two: those which fall on the rates, these being essentially the same as the functions performed by London boroughs with the exception of (i) Port Health Authority functions which are assigned by statute to the City and (ii) the City Police; secondly, those which are financed from the City's own resources – these include notably the maintenance of markets (except Spitalfields) and open spaces such as Epping Forest; educational activities (the City is not an education authority but maintains the City of London School, the City of London School for Girls and the Guildhall School of Music and Drama); and responsibility for four Thames bridges, London Bridge,[1] Tower Bridge, Southwark Bridge and Blackfriars Bridge.

The Greater London Council. With a population of $7\frac{3}{4}$ million, an area of 620 square miles, a current gross revenue expenditure of nearly £200 million, and a total staff of nearly 50,000,[2] the G.L.C. is a giant among local authorities. Yet in many ways its constitution and organisation resemble those of a county council. It differs significantly in the number of members. Lancashire C.C., for example, the largest county council, responsible for a population of 2,400,000, has 166 councillors and aldermen. The Greater London Council has only 100 councillors and sixteen aldermen. Admittedly, the G.L.C. does not have the same range of functions as a county council since it is not responsible for the personal social services or for services such as libraries. It does, nevertheless, have a considerable range of functions for which it has instituted an elaborate committee structure.

When it was first constituted the G.L.C. set up fourteen standing committees. This structure closely followed the L.C.C. pattern, as was perhaps only to be expected in view of the fact that a high proportion of the members of the G.L.C. had previously served on the L.C.C.[3] These fourteen committees comprised, apart from the usual general committees (Finance, General Purposes, Supplies, etc.) separate committees for the Ambulance Service, Fire Brigade, Highways and Traffic, Housing, Licensing, New and Expanding Towns, Parks and Smallholdings, Planning and Communications and Public Health Services. Apart from the Housing and Highways and Traffic Committees, all fourteen committees were composed exclusively of members of the Council. Since no committee had fewer

[1] In 1967 the City Corporation sold the old London Bridge and began to replace it with a new bridge estimated to cost £4.5 million; the whole of this cost is being met by the Corporation's Bridge House Estates Fund.

[2] Excluding in both cases the Inner London Education Authority (expenditure £60 million, staff 60,000).

[3] Rather more than one-third of the councillors elected to the G.L.C. in 1964 were members of the L.C.C.

than twelve members and many committees, like the Council itself, met fortnightly, there was a considerable burden of work for the 116 members of the Council. This was particularly so in the case of the Leader of the Council and the Leader of the Opposition[1] and of the committee chairmen.

There were two ways in which changes might be sought in the position. One was in the direction of streamlining the committee structure, the other in compensating members for the burden of work which they had to perform. Both these approaches have been pursued by the G.L.C. Indeed, it is probably true to say that the original committee structure was regarded as an interim measure simply to get the new authority into being. On the question of compensation to members, the Council were in a difficulty; the Government had rejected proposals during the passage of the London Government Bill that members or committee chairmen of the G.L.C. should be paid a fee or salary, on the grounds that this was something to be determined in relation of local government generally. And the Government-appointed committee on the Management of Local Government (Maud Committee) in an interim report in 1966 showed an unwillingness to change the tradition of unpaid service so firmly established in local government.[2] The G.L.C. therefore pressed for and eventually secured an improvement in the terms on which members could claim compensation for loss of earnings caused by attendance on Council business.[3]

In 1966 the G.L.C. set up a special committee on procedure to examine in the first place the Council's committee structure. Some relatively minor changes took place meanwhile[4] but this was the first attempt to devise a structure appropriate to the unique powers exercised by the G.L.C. The special committee also had to take into account the report of the Maud Committee on Management of Local Government which recommended among other things that local authorities should appoint a management board with a limited membership drawn from both the majority and minority parties on the council as a policy-initiating body; that more power should be delegated to chief officers; and that committees should be deliberative bodies and fewer in number.[5]

[1] As in the L.C.C., the leader of the majority party on the Council (Leader of the Council), and the leader of the minority party (Leader of the Opposition) have a recognised role under the G.L.C.'s Standing Orders.

[2] Printed in the Committee's *Report*, Vol. 1 (H.M.S.O., 1967), pp. 167–74.

[3] On this see G.L.C. Minutes, March 14, 1967, pp. 203–4. The terms were not as generous as the G.L.C. would have wished (ibid., January 28, 1969).

[4] e.g. the Fire and Ambulance Committees were merged in 1967.

[5] *Report*, Vol. 1 (H.M.S.O., 1967), paras. 151, 158, 162, 166, 169.

In considering the changes which the G.L.C. has made as a result of the proposals of its special committee on procedure, one point should be noted about the original list of committees. Most of the functional committees have an obvious relationship to a particular function or group of functions performed by the G.L.C. The title of two committees, however, Highways and Traffic, and Planning and Communications, suggests that a rather different basis was intended here, namely, that the first should be responsible for the G.L.C.'s executive powers in highways and traffic management, and the second for the whole field of planning including the planning of the road network. But in practice a more complicated system of joint sub-committees of the two committees grew up to deal with the many questions of mutual concern.[1]

The committee on procedure based its proposals on the proposition that the G.L.C. had two roles: to decide policy on long-term planning; and to carry out executive responsibilities. It thought that these separate roles should be reflected in the committee structure in place of the existing functional basis. The proposals, approved by the Council on July 23, 1968, provided for three types of committee –

(i) Major policy committees: a *Leader's Co-ordinating Committee* to ensure regular policy co-ordination; a *Policy Steering Committee* to be concerned with medium- and long-term objectives for all G.L.C. services; and a *Strategic Planning Committee* to be responsible for the Greater London Development Plan and generally for the medium- and long-term planning carried out by the Highways and Traffic and the Planning and Communications Committees.

(ii) Nine executive committees, involving some regrouping of existing committees.[2] Perhaps the most interesting of these is the *Planning and Transportation Committee*, combining the short-term planning and executive functions of the Highways and Traffic and Planning and Communications Committees.

(iii) Special committees: including a *Scrutiny Committee* to investigate the working and activities of the Council; the *Procedure Committee*; and a *Staff Appeals Committee*.

Apart from the separation of policy and executive committees, the most interesting of the new arrangements is the creation of the Leader's Co-ordinating Committee as an official committee of the

---

[1] See below, page 107.

[2] For example, a Public Services Committee was to take over not only public health functions (ambulance service, drainage, sewerage, refuse disposal, etc.) but also the fire brigade and licensing; in fact, it was to be a residual functional committee.

Council. This is a committee of leading members of the majority party only, under the chairmanship of the Leader of the Council. It existed before but purely as a party committee; it was not therefore serviced by the Clerk's Department, and could not draw on the advice of the chief officers. Now, as a full committee of the Council, it will be able to take a possibly decisive role in the future development of the G.L.C. It is the Council's answer to the Maud Committee's management board which was specifically rejected as inapplicable to the G.L.C.'s situation.

But although the new structure appears to be a sensible improvement on the previous structure, it leaves a number of questions unanswered. In particular, the relationships between the Council and the new committees and between the committees themselves may cause problems; there may well, for example, be overlap not only between the Strategic Planning and Planning and Transportation Committees, but also on occasions between the Policy Steering and the Strategic Planning and other committees. It is here presumably that the Leader's Co-ordinating Committee may well have one of its most important roles, but much will turn on how the new machinery is worked in practice, and here the differing attitudes of different leaders and indeed of different parties will be interesting to observe.

The committee structure also needs to be looked at in relation to the G.L.C.'s departmental structure, and to other aspects of the internal management. Seventeen departments each under a chief officer were established when the G.L.C. was set up. Like the original committee structure, this departmental structure owed a great deal to the experience of previous authorities, particularly the L.C.C. Most indeed of the departments call for no comment, as they can be paralleled in a great many other local authorities. Thus, the Treasurer's, Valuer's, Architect's and Director of Housing's Departments have obvious functions. Separate departments were established for planning (under a Director of Planning) and for highways and transportation (under a Director of Highways and Transportation), the latter's title indicating the rather wider scope intended for it than for the corresponding committee. A separate establishment department (under a Director of Establishments) and a legal and Parliamentary department (under a Solicitor and Parliamentary Officer) were established, no doubt in recognition of the fact that the Clerk of the Council would have a heavy task as chief administrative and co-ordinating officer without being burdened with these additional responsibilities.

The special committee on procedure has not yet issued a comprehensive report on departmental organisation. The changes which

F

have been made since 1965 in the G.L.C.'s internal management
other than the committee structure nevertheless indicate the direction in which the Council is moving. There has been greater delegation of powers to committee chairman and officers, the Clerk's role
as chief administrative officer has been strengthened and he is now
designated 'Director-General and Clerk to the Council'; and efforts
have been made to provide better machinery for co-ordination at
officer level.[1] Some of these changes might well have taken place in
any case given the general climate of opinion stimulated by the
Maud Committee's report. But it is likely that the G.L.C. would
sooner or later have had to look closely at its internal arrangements
in view of its peculiar range of responsibilities and the problems of
co-ordination inherent in them.[2]

The London boroughs. The boroughs, having a more conventional
range of functions than the G.L.C., did not have quite the same problems of organising their committee and departmental structure. The
Maud Committee found that in 1965 most had relatively few committees but the number of departments varied from five to eighteen.[3]
Since then, in common with other authorities, the London boroughs
have been seeking ways of improving their internal organisation, and,
as new authorities, they have probably been readier to innovate than
many older authorities.[4]

Thus although rarely pioneers, so far at least, London boroughs
have adopted many current ideas. Wandsworth, for example, in 1968
appointed a chief executive in place of their town clerk who had
retired; in this they followed places like Newcastle and Basildon,
as well as the recommendations of the Maud Committee. One of the
tasks of the chief executive, before he resigned after less than a year
in office, was to streamline the committee and departmental structure.
Haringey similarly were actively engaged in 1969 in a major review
of their administration involving a reduction in the number of com-

---

[1] For example, a chief officers' board has been set up consisting of the director-
general and clerk as chairman, with the treasurer and director of establishments
as the other permanent members. Other chief officers attend when their department's affairs are under consideration. The board advises on major policy
proposals and long-term planning programmes (see G.L.C. Minutes, October 22,
1968).

[2] In July 1969 the G.L.C. decided to merge the planning and highways and
transportation departments.

[3] *Committee on the Management of Local Government*, Vol. 5, 'Local Government Administration in England and Wales', pp. 221–2, 539, 573, 588, 595.

[4] See *Recent Reforms in the Management Structure of Local Authorities –
the London Boroughs* (Institute of Local Government Studies, University of
Birmingham, Occasional Paper 2, 1969); also Occasional Paper 1 dealing with
county boroughs.

mittees to eight and the establishment of a five-man directorate under a chief executive to be responsible for co-ordination and forward planning of services. Greenwich had earlier carried out a drastic reduction of committees and departments; departments are now grouped so that, for example, a director of technical services is now responsible for all engineering, planning and architectural work.

Interesting as these and other examples are of the changes now taking place, they do not differ greatly from similar efforts being made by local authorities elsewhere. The external relations of the London boroughs, however, are of interest in a way that differs significantly from what is to be found outside Greater London. It must be remembered that one feature of the new system of London government was that it created thirty-two authorities with identical powers[1] and status. Moreover, all these authorities had a common relationship with the G.L.C. in view of the sharing of functions between them. In this situation there was scope for co-operation and co-ordination of effort if the system was to work with reasonable smoothness. Hence the importance of the *London Boroughs Association* (L.B.A.) which has taken a leading part in promoting such arrangements.

Originally called the London Boroughs Committee[2] (the name was changed in 1966 to what was considered a more appropriate title) the L.B.A. held its inaugural meeting on June 24, 1964; its constitution (under general local government powers) was laid down in September 1964, its objects being:

(a) To protect and advance the powers, interests, rights and privileges of the constituent Councils and to watch over those powers, interests, rights and privileges as they may be affected by legislation, or proposed legislation.

(b) To discuss questions of London government and to advise and assist the constituent Councils in the administration of their powers and duties.

(c) To express the views of the Association and to consult with appropriate bodies or persons whenever deemed advisable. Provided that the Association shall not have power to bind or commit a constituent authority.

(The proviso in the last section of (c) should be particularly noted.)

[1] With of course the important exception that education is a function only of the outer London boroughs.
[2] The following account is based on *The Lessons of the London Government Reforms* (H.M.S.O., 1968), pp. 17–21, by permission of the Controller of Her Majesty's Stationery Office.

The work of the Association is at present carried out through four committees – General Purposes, Works, Social Services and Education. Each council has one representative on each of the first three committees (a total of ninety-nine with the inclusion of the City) and these members constitute the Association; Town Clerks are the Honorary Secretaries of each committee and also of the Association. The Education Committee has one representative of each of the twenty outer London boroughs who are not full members of the Association unless they happen to be on one of the other committees. All four committees are served by advisory bodies of chief officers, two members of each of which attend committee meetings as representatives.

Much of the work of the Association (which is financed by contributions from constituent councils) is concerned with relations with the G.L.C. and with the common problems of the boroughs. But it is also the recognised channel of communication, e.g. with Government departments, on borough interests so far as they relate only to London, the Association of Municipal Corporations dealing with questions of wider implication. The advantages not only to the boroughs but also to the G.L.C. in having a common meeting-point for discussion of matters of mutual concern have been particularly evident in planning and housing, two shared functions which have raised thorny problems.[1]

The London Boroughs' Association is the chief agency for co-operation among the boroughs, but two other bodies, the London Boroughs' Management Services Unit (L.B.M.S.U.) and the London Boroughs' Training Committee (Social Services), also play important roles in serving the common needs of the boroughs. Unlike the L.B.A., which is a voluntary association of local authorities, these two have been set up under the statutory powers[2] which permit local authorities to establish joint committees.

The L.B.M.S.U. is descended from the Metropolitan Boroughs' Organisation and Methods Committee. Unlike the L.B.A., not all the London boroughs are members, some maintaining their own O and M units.[3] There are at present eighteen boroughs in membership, of which nine are in inner London, i.e. the former L.C.C. area. Each borough is represented by one member on the L.B.M.S.U. and there is an advisory body of chief officers. The Unit is headed by a Director, and has an O and M and Operational Research Division, a Work Study Division, and a Computer Division. The Unit has a total staff

[1] See below, pp. 98–100.
[2] Local Government Act, 1933, Section 91.
[3] e.g. Bexley, Enfield and Havering.

of over 300 and an annual budget of more than half a million pounds.[1]

Among the tasks undertaken by the Unit perhaps the most ambitious is a survey, designed to extend over five years, of the main departments of all the constituent authorities. The study includes consideration of overall management, committee structure, and interdepartmental relations. Work-study techniques, including the introduction of bonus schemes, have already been applied in several boroughs to a number of operations performed by manual labour. The Computer Division operates two joint computer schemes for groups of boroughs; a number of boroughs which are not members of the Unit operate their own computers.

The Unit does not work exclusively for the London boroughs. It also undertakes assignments for outside authorities on repayment, thus enabling it to employ extra staff and spread the cost of overheads.

The London Boroughs' Training Committee (Social Services) was formed to contend with the serious shortage of trained social workers with which the new authorities were faced, and held its first meeting in December 1964. All but three of the thirty-two boroughs are members. The Committee consists of one representative from each constituent Authority, with a Town Clerk and a Borough Treasurer as honorary secretary and treasurer, an advisory body of three Medical Officers of Health, three Chief Welfare Officers and three Children's Officers, and a Director of Training. Courses have been organised for assistant child care officers, health visitor field work instructors, school nurses and education welfare officers among others. The Committee has also held seminars and conferences. To give confidence to potential applicants for residential work, a pre-recruitment course was introduced and to attract back married women with training and experience a 're-entry course' has been organised.

The L.B.A., L.B.M.S.U. and the London Boroughs' Training Committee are all formal organisations constituted under the general powers of local authorities. The London Government Act, 1963, does, however, specifically permit the G.L.C., the boroughs and the City Corporation to make arrangements among themselves for mutual help and co-operation.[2] Whether or not inspired by this provision, the boroughs have made a number of such arrangements. Some of these arrangements can be closely paralleled by similar arrangements among other local authorities. For example, the boroughs operate in three groups as the London Housing Consortium for the use of industrialised building.

[1] See *Annual Report*, London Boroughs' Management Services Unit, 1967–8.
[2] Section 5 (3).

Other arrangements, however, arise from the special circumstances of London government. There is, for example, a Central London Planning Conference consisting of a number of boroughs in the Central Area which exists to consider problems of mutual interest. Again, because of the difficulty of recruiting trained staff, there are several consortia operating the boroughs' weights and measures functions (e.g. Kingston upon Thames, Merton and Sutton; Ealing and Brent; Greenwich, Lambeth, Lewisham, Southwark and Wandsworth). Westminster and Kensington & Chelsea operate a joint computer committee, independently of the L.B.M.S.U. In some cases, the G.L.C. also has a role in some of these arrangements, particularly in planning questions; for example, a consortium of the G.L.C., Westminster and Camden was formed to carry out the redevelopment of Covent Garden, the cost being shared in the proportions G.L.C. 50 per cent, Westminster 35 per cent and Camden 15 per cent.

The L.B.A. itself remains the chief means whereby an agreed policy may be reached on matters which affect all the boroughs. But it is important to remember that it can only recommend courses of action to constituent authorities, and has no power to enforce its decisions. Nevertheless, many matters coming before the L.B.A. are ones on which it is essential for the boroughs to co-operate, and on these matters there has generally been agreement on the course to be followed. This is particularly true of the many detailed problems which arose initially over the transfer of services from the old county authorities to the boroughs. For example, there was the problem of admission of old people to the large homes which the boroughs inherited in the L.C.C. area. Under the new system, one borough became responsible for running each home but one or more other boroughs shares its accommodation. It was agreed at an early meeting of the L.B.A. that the Chief Welfare Officer of Camden should undertake the duties of Bed Controller for these large homes to overcome difficulties in allocating places arising from the shared arrangements.

Typical of the opportunities provided by the new system as well as the difficulties is the problem of scales of payment in the welfare services. Charges to be paid by recipients or relatives who have a statutory liability to pay for services rendered have always tended to vary not only as between authorities but also as between services. The L.B.A. took the initiative in attempting to establish a common assessment scale throughout Greater London, and in 1967 recommended a scheme which although it would not achieve complete uniformity would go a long way towards that goal.

Again, an interesting example of co-operation in connection with public control functions is provided by the agreements that individual boroughs should be responsible for keeping central registers of prosecutions under the various Acts concerned, viz.

Weights and Measures	City of London
Employment Agencies	
Nursing Agencies	
Theatre Agencies	
Pool Betting Agencies	Westminster
Massage Establishments	
Refreshment Houses	
Food and Drugs	
Food Hygiene	Lambeth

In addition, Westminster keep a central register of refusals of registration under the National Assistance Act (Old People's Homes) and the Nursing Homes and Nursery and Child Minders Acts.

A problem of a rather different kind arose in the field of finance. A Rate Equalisation Scheme had existed in the County of London under which the six or seven richest metropolitan boroughs and the City made contributions to the remaining boroughs. This helped to reduce the variation in rates needing to be levied in the different authorities. The scheme was continued as an interim measure operating in inner London after April 1, 1965, but because of the changes introduced by the 1963 Act, particularly in the distribution of functions, there were anomalies, including the fact that the City now became a receiving authority. It was clear, therefore, that the scheme would have to be reviewed. Accordingly, the L.B.A. invited an outside consultant, Professor A. R. Ilersic of London University, to consider whether a scheme of equalisation was desirable under the new system, and, if so, whether it should apply to the whole of Greater London.

In his report,[1] Professor Ilersic suggested a new scheme applicable to the whole of Greater London. He argued that the existing scheme was based too much on needs as measured by expenditure and not enough on resources. He therefore proposed a scheme which would try to take into account both the differing needs and the differing resources of the London boroughs, although he recognised that it was not easy to measure either of these precisely.

He suggested that resources should be measured primarily by taking the aggregate of non-domestic rateable value in each borough, on the grounds that help was mainly needed for the domestic ratepayer.

[1] *Rate Equalisation in London*, published by the Institute of Municipal Treasurers and Accountants (1968).

To this should, however, be added the aggregate of domestic r.v. of property rated at £200 or more since he thought that wealthier domestic ratepayers could be expected to make some contribution; correspondingly, there should be a deduction for the aggregate r.v. on very low-rated property. On the sum total thus arrived at for each borough he proposed a contribution of 10 per cent (2s. in the pound) which, on 1967 figures, gave a total contribution of £38 million.

He suggested allocation of this sum by means of a formula based on the needs element in the Government's Rate Support Grant, but making greater allowance for such factors as the proportion of children and old people in the population of each borough.

The net result of these proposals was that four authorities in inner London and four in outer London would contribute more than they received, particularly high net contributions being made by Westminster (£8 million) and the City (£4·3 million). Boroughs receiving significantly more than they contributed included Lewisham (£1·6 million), Wandsworth (£1·6 million) and Southwark (£1·4 million). In Outer London only Bromley (£641,000) and Havering (£561,000) received more than £500,000 net. On the other hand, largely because of the very large contributions by Westminster and the City, outer London as a whole gained £4 million from inner London.

Professor Ilersic's scheme was on the whole acceptable to the L.B.A. and most of the boroughs, but met objections from the Ministry of Housing and Local Government. It was, however, introduced in 1968, but may be modified as a result of subsequent discussions.

As these examples illustrate, the degree of co-operation between the London boroughs is on a scale which exceeds that usually to be found among a group of contiguous local authorities; and in this co-operation a key role is played by the London Boroughs Association. Co-operation has been made easier by the fact that thirty-two new authorities were simultaneously brought into being with approximately similar size, status and functions, each responsible for provision of services in a part of the built-up area of London. There was thus an obvious need for co-operation if the system was to work smoothly, not only in those areas of administration which were exclusively the province of the boroughs, but also in order that the boroughs should have common policies in matters which affected their relationship with the Greater London Council.

But this is only part of the story. It was not inevitable that the boroughs should come together in the way they have done. One should therefore pay tribute to the far-sightedness of those members and officers of local authorities in London who saw the need and worked for the creation at an early stage of what became the L.B.A.

Undoubtedly, the main impetus came from the Metropolitan Boroughs' Standing Joint Committee, without whose existence as an example and precedent the creation of the L.B.A would have been much more difficult.

There is also a deeper issue raised by the present situation. Some of the co-operative arrangements which the boroughs have devised, e.g. the consortia for weights and measures functions, might be interpreted by critics of the new system as indications either of the disadvantages of dispersing functions from large authorities to much smaller ones or of the fact that the boroughs are too small to carry out the range of functions allotted to them. The issue probably arises most acutely with education in the outer London boroughs; in a number of instances boroughs have made arrangements with neighbouring boroughs to share specialised staff and premises, whereas under the previous county system the authority was large enough to provide both out of its own resources.

There is no simple answer to such questions, but the following points are relevant. First, the optimum size of authority for different services varies; in creating multi-purpose authorities, therefore, it is almost inevitable that such authorities will be better equipped to perform some functions than others. Secondly, it follows from this that it is necessary to take a broad view of the performance of authorities before deciding whether the system is good or bad. Thirdly, it does not necessarily follow that sharing arrangements between authorities are inferior to exclusive performance; it may be, for example, that an equally good service can be provided in the former case and at the same time other advantages secured, e.g. smaller authorities may be more responsive to local needs.

These questions will be referred to again after an examination has been made of the working of a number of important services under the new system. Meanwhile, we now consider what impact the new authorities have made on the general public and, in particular, the voting public.

B. REACTIONS OF THE PUBLIC[1]

Elections

There have been four elections for the new authorities since the 1963 Act, for the G.L.C. in 1964 and 1967, and for the boroughs in 1964 and 1968. A study of the voting figures in these elections is of interest

[1] We are indebted to the Controller of Her Majesty's Stationery Office for permission to base this section on material contained in *The Lessons of the London Government Reforms* (H.M.S.O., 1968), pp. 38–44.

for any indications which they give of changes in voting habits. They are unlikely, however, to answer directly the question whether the new system has attracted a greater degree of public participation than the old. Apart from other factors, there is an increasing tendency to conduct local elections on party political lines, as has long been true of London. The extent of voting may therefore reflect more current political trends at the national political level than concern with the local situation.

Moreover, active canvassing by the party machines does not necessarily increase the turn-out. There is evidence that in areas where one party has a large preponderance, the efforts of that party are confined to securing a sufficient turn-out of supporters to ensure a majority, while the other party may not bother to canvass at all, making use of its activists in more marginal seats.[1]

In the G.L.C. election of 1964 the average turn-out was 44·2 compared with 36·4 and 38·6 respectively in the London and Middlesex County Councils elections of 1961. This seems to show a markedly greater interest in the Greater London Council election, especially since in the neighbouring counties of Kent, Essex and Surrey the turn-out went down by more than 5 per cent in the elections there in 1965. Indeed it was precisely to the boroughs formerly in these adjoining counties that this increased interest was very largely confined. Of the twelve inner London boroughs (those comprising the former County of London) eight had a turn-out within 2 per cent of what it had been in the 1961 L.C.C. election: in one it was lower, by 4 per cent, and in only three was it higher (by 7 per cent in two cases and 5 per cent in the other). In the outer boroughs by contrast there were increases everywhere, ranging from 9 to 18 per cent.

In the 1967 elections however, the turn-out decreased by 3·2 to 41·0 per cent, while in Kent, Essex and Surrey there was an increase of 10 per cent, which suggests that interest in the G.L.C. as a new authority was waning. However, the contrast between inner and outer London still persisted: in the former the average turn-out was 33·8 per cent, in the latter 48·2 per cent. Although in five outer boroughs the percentage increased over 1964, it was also there that the greatest reductions took place (Barking 9·3 per cent, Harrow 9 per cent).

The explanation of the 1967 figures lies in the political situation. The five boroughs in outer London with increases were all marginal – in two a small Conservative majority was increased, in three there

---

[1] For the two safest Labour seats in the G.L.C. elections the turnouts were 22·4 and 23·8 in 1964 and 20·6 and 19·8 in 1967; for the safest Conservative seat, 38·1 in 1964 and 32·7 in 1967.

was a change from Labour to Conservative. The two with the large decreases were both safe party seats – Barking Labour, Harrow Conservative. In these two boroughs the Conservative vote remained roughly stationary, the Labour vote fell by between a third and a half. Over Greater London as a whole the Conservative vote rose by 176,000, but the Labour vote fell by 339,200 (resulting in a Conservative majority of elected members of sixty-four in place of a Labour majority of twenty-eight).

It is thus fairly clear that the decline in turn-out was mainly due to a large number of abstentions by those who had voted Labour in 1964, and highly probable that such abstentions were deliberate. In other words, non-voting was used as a means of political expression short of voting for the other side, as happens from time to time in parliamentary divisions.

But this swing from Labour was a national phenomenon due to disappointment with Labour's performance in national government and had little or nothing to do with local issues in London or elsewhere. Because Greater London is the largest local authority it is regarded as a political prize by both the main national parties, which back the candidates with the party machinery. This is certainly a major factor in the comparatively large voting turn-out.

That the average Londoner does not cast his vote at a G.L.C. election in the knowledge of the issues and personalities involved is shown by a survey commissioned by the G.L.C. and by a significant occurrence at the last election.

The survey undertaken by Mass Observation Ltd. covered a random sample of all adults over twenty-one on the electoral rolls. The number in the sample was 2,630 of whom 70 per cent were actually interviewed.

The report of the survey indicated that as many as one third of Londoners did not know what the letters G.L.C. stood for. One in ten were unaware that they lived in Greater London and one in four did not know in which of the new London boroughs they lived. And while more than half correctly named their Members of Parliament, only one in fifty could name one of their representatives on the Greater London Council. There was widespread lack of knowledge of what services the rates pay for and over 80 per cent of Londoners did not realise that more than one authority receives the money.

Considerable confusion existed concerning which services were run by the G.L.C. No one major service was correctly associated with the Council by more than two in five people, while a substantial proportion believed that certain other services were the Council's responsibility when, in fact, they were not.

The significant occurrence was that in one London borough two candidates stood with the same name though slightly differently spelt – one Labour (a man of considerable eminence in London Government for several years) and one Liberal. This being a four-member constituency, three other candidates from these parties were also standing. The Labour candidate with the same name received 6,000 less votes than the other Labour candidates, the Liberal candidate with the same name 6,000 more than the other Liberal candidates (more than twice their number). Clearly 6,000 electors did not know for whom they were voting and indeed their task was not made any easier by the fact that in this four-member constituency they were confronted by a list of twenty names.

The blame for this lack of knowledge may not all rest with the voter – of this more is said below under 'Public Relations'.

The London Borough Elections of 1964 presented a different picture. Here the average turn-out was 35·7 per cent against 44·2 per cent for the G.L.C. Moreover in the whole of Greater London there was only one borough (Enfield, 2·6 per cent) in which the turn-out was more than 2 per cent higher that it had been in the previous election for the constituent authorities. In one ward of one borough (Hackney) less than 10 per cent of the electorate voted. By contrast the average turn-out increased by 5·7 per cent in Essex boroughs and district councils and by 3·3 per cent in Surrey. In Kent there was a decrease but only of 1·4 per cent.

Clearly the emergence of a new type of local authority in the form of the new London boroughs excited no interest in the average elector.[1] For this there are two probable explanations. First the borough elections followed very shortly after the G.L.C. which stole their thunder as being a bigger and more dramatic affair. Secondly, the voters, who could grasp the idea of a bigger L.C.C., were now, save in the case of Harrow, confronted with the unknown. They might know their Poplar as a local authority, but Tower Hamlets was something alien to them.

A somewhat different picture was presented by the 1968 borough elections. In the first place, they represented a huge electoral land-slide. The average swing from Labour to Conservative was over 20 per cent and in nine wards was over 40 per cent, with the result that Labour, instead of having control of twenty-one of the thirty-two boroughs, was left with only four.

The interesting point here is that the result was not due to ab-

---

[1] This is conspicuously the case with Harrow, where the functions of the authority changed but its boundaries did not, and there was a drop of 5 per cent in the turn-out.

stentions. The average turn-out was almost identical in the two elections: 35·7 in 1964, 35·8 in 1968. But on this occasion the decline was
in the outer boroughs, from about 41 per cent to just under 40 per
cent, while in inner London it was up from about 27 to 29 per cent.
Thus in Islington, where 29,000 voted in 1964, 35,000 voted in 1968,
and in the Hackney ward with the vote of less than 10 per cent in
1964, 1,147 (some 14 per cent) voted as against 715.

It is clear then that in the 1968 election not only were there Labour
abstentions, but also some change of sides, and that in inner London
some voted who had not voted before.

As in the case of the G.L.C. 1967 election, the huge electoral swing
was almost certainly due to discontent with Labour as a national
government rather than to any local government factors.

In conclusion it may be said with regard to the G.L.C. that more
voters in the outer boroughs take the opportunity of recording their
votes in elections in which they are regarded as Londoners, than did
in the county elections. It looks, however, as if interest may be waning
somewhat. It may also be waning in the borough elections, at the
same time as it is showing an increase in inner London. But this
movement may be due to the fact that Conservative canvassers
concentrated their efforts on inner London in 1968. What seems
clear, however, is that the London voter in casting his vote has
his eye on national rather than local issues.[1]

Public relations

It was suggested above that ignorance about the significance of his
vote is not altogether the fault of the elector. Local authorities often
give little information to the public about what they are doing. The
new London authorities have however shown an early awareness of
their responsibilities in this respect.

The G.L.C. at the end of 1965 appointed a firm as their public
relations consultants, and this firm, after commissioning the survey
mentioned above, recommended the establishment of a public
information branch in the Clerk's department. Their proposals,
with some modifications, were adopted and the Public Information
Branch came into full operation in April 1967. Among its productions
was *Capital Service* (later called *Greater London Services*), an extremely useful guide to the local government services of Greater
London, but this had a circulation of only 20,000 in a population of
8 million. You can bring water to the horse but you can't make him
drink.

[1] Cf. the conclusion by Peter Fletcher in *Voting in Cities* (London, Macmillan,
1967), pp. 319–21.

An example of public relations on the part of an individual department was given by the Highways and Transportation Department in connection with the disruption and inconvenience caused to whole neighbourhoods by the construction of the Western Avenue extension and part of the West Cross route. 20,000 letters were delivered by hand explaining the purpose of the road and the general timing of the work. All residents were given the address and telephone number of the resident engineer and encouraged to get in touch with him in case of difficulty, and also the telephone extension at County Hall to which any particular problem could be notified for immediate investigation.

The boroughs. Most of these also now have their public relations officers, and in fact more than a third of the authorities in the country employing public relations staff are in Greater London. This development has been in response to a general feeling of the need to make the public aware of what the boroughs are and what they do.

In addition the L.B.A. decided on the issue of an 80-page booklet on the work of the London boroughs as a complement to the G.L.C.'s *Greater London Services.* The compilation of the booklet was put in the hands of a group of borough P.R.O.s but the project has been deferred in present economic circumstances.

Individual authorities have adopted various methods of keeping the public informed of their activities. Lewisham, for example, hold an open forum from time to time. That on housing produced an audience of 200. Haringey is one of the boroughs producing a quarterly review. Among other features a recent issue contained precise information as to the functions performed by the G.L.C. and the boroughs, and an invitation to attend Council meetings – 'Hear your business discussed. Agendas supplied. Seating for 100. Free car parking.' The *Barking Record*, a well-produced and illustrated small quarterly magazine, is highly entertaining as well as informative.

All the boroughs admit the press to council meetings, and all supply the press with agendas beforehand. The question of affording admission to committee meetings also has been considered in certain boroughs, but this involves difficulty where publicity given to matters under negotiation might prejudice the interests of the Council. One borough holds press conferences half-way through its committee cycle so that information does not have to wait for the Council agenda. Another circulates the results of committee meetings after the meetings.

One disadvantage from the publicity angle experienced both by the G.L.C. and the boroughs is that, unlike most of the major provincial cities, London has no morning daily of its own, all the dailies in fact being national organs. The two London evening papers to some extent fill the gap and give prominence to specifically London news, but their status and influence is hardly that of the great dailies.

In conclusion it should be said that with the consensus of opinion moving in favour of larger authorities, and with the tendency towards fewer committees concerned with policy and more delegation to officials, more and more matters of concern to the public are as it were pushed out of sight. It is therefore all the more important that the electorate should be kept informed of what is going on through all those methods which come under the term of public relations.

Chapter V

PLANNING, HIGHWAYS AND TRAFFIC: THE G.L.C. AND THE BOROUGHS

THE GENERAL POSITION

As was suggested earlier, an essential part of the case for a Greater London authority and hence for a fundamental change in the existing system of local government in London was the need to plan for the built-up area as a whole. This required not only a strategic land-use plan for Greater London, but an authority which could effectively deal with London's traffic problems. Clearly, this implied close links between the physical planning, including the planning of the road network; and the carrying out of traffic measures. Public transport, too, which was not considered by the Herbert Commission and not touched by the 1963 Act, was vitally concerned in any policies which were evolved for highways and traffic. Looked at from the angle of the G.L.C., therefore, it is useful to consider planning, highways and traffic together, not only because of the links between them but also because, apart from housing, most other functions of the G.L.C., although important in themselves, do not add up to an argument for a large authority of this type.[1] The G.L.C. is a strategic planning authority, taken in the widest sense, or it is nothing.

Three other sets of authorities are also involved. There are first two major government departments, the Ministry of Housing and Local Government, and the Ministry of Transport. The latter since the 1963 Act seems to have moved in the direction of giving the G.L.C. greater powers. Secondly, there are the London boroughs who naturally view planning and highways from a quite different point of view from the G.L.C. and whose responsibilities in these fields are not necessarily so closely linked together as are the G.L.C.'s. Finally there are important traffic functions exercised by the Metropolitan and City of London Police forces; for them, too, these functions are only a part and not necessarily the most important part of their total functions.

---

[1] Housing is briefly referred to on p. 169; but the fire brigade, main drainage, refuse disposal and other G.L.C. services are more in the nature of services which may conveniently be given to a Greater London authority established on other grounds.

Even within the G.L.C., as was shown above, separate departments and separate committees were originally set up for planning on the one hand and traffic and highways on the other,[1] although the committee structure has recently been changed.[2]

Certain general points need to be made about the position in London. First, it is not static. Partly as a result of the 1963 Act and partly for other reasons there has been much re-examination of the powers and responsibilities of the different authorities, particularly in the traffic and transport fields, which has led among other things to legislation providing for the G.L.C. to assume responsibility for London Transport.[3] Secondly, even within the framework laid down by the 1963 Act there has been a continuous process of redefining the relative spheres of action of the G.L.C. and the boroughs, and this process is still going on, particularly with regard to planning powers. Thirdly, we are here dealing with essentially long-term plans and activities. The Greater London Development Plan for example, was not due to be submitted to the Minister until July 31, 1969, and is not likely to be approved for some time after that – the draft statement published by the G.L.C. in March 1969 suggests that it is only a first stage in drawing up a strategic plan for London. Lastly, it needs to be stressed how much the new arrangements differ not only from those which existed before in London, but from those to be found anywhere else in the country; this will be commented on further below.

The consequence of this situation is that it is not possible to analyse directly the performance of functions under the old system and compare it with the new. In the case, for example, of the children's service, exactly the same powers and duties are now exercised by the London boroughs as were previously performed by the different counties and county boroughs in the area, and it is therefore possible, at least in principle, to see what effect this change has had.

With planning and, still more, with traffic there are both new authorities and new functions. Apart from the specially commissioned Plan for Greater London by Professor Abercrombie published in 1945, no person or body had until 1965 the job of keeping under review the planning needs of Greater London as a whole; in so far as this duty was performed it was done by the Minister of Housing and Local Government, but only to the extent that he was able to co-ordinate the various separate plans produced by the nine local planning

---

[1] Planning and Communications Committee and Planning Department; Highways and Traffic Committee and Highways and Transportation Department.
[2] See above, p. 80.
[3] The Transport (London) Act, 1969; see below, p. 111.

G

authorities[1] in the area under the Town and Country Planning Act, 1947. Under the new system introduced by the 1963 Act the G.L.C. has assumed this responsibility.

In the traffic field the London and Home Counties Traffic Advisory Committee set up under the London Traffic Act, 1924, was for long the only body with a wide oversight of London's traffic problems, and, as its name implies, it had no executive powers. In 1960 faced with the mounting problems of London traffic the Minister of Transport set up within his department a London Traffic Management Unit, charged with the duty of proposing and, after consultation with the various local bodies concerned, carrying into effect schemes for regulating traffic in London.[2] The effect of the 1963 Act was to transfer by and large the powers of the Minister to the G.L.C. In examining the present system of London government in these fields particular attention will therefore be paid to two aspects: first, how the new authorities have set about the task of dealing with these novel functions; secondly, what difficulties and limitations on the effectiveness of the system have been disclosed in practice.

THE G.L.C. AND THE BOROUGHS IN PLANNING

It was obvious that following the passing of the 1963 Act a great deal of detailed work needed to be done in fixing the precise responsibilities of the G.L.C. and the boroughs in planning. In 1964 and the early part of 1965 there was a good deal of discussion between the Ministry of Housing and Local Government, the G.L.C. and the boroughs on what should be put in the Regulations dealing with the development plans and the control of planning applications.[3] Several points became clear at this early stage. One, which was constantly emphasized by the Ministry, was the need for close co-operation between the G.L.C. and the boroughs if the new system was to work. To this end, a joint working party of officers of the G.L.C. and the boroughs was set up to consider matters of mutual concern. Their reports have covered a wide variety of topics and have generally been accepted by the parties concerned. For example, the twelfth report

[1] That is, the county councils of London, Middlesex, Essex, Surrey, Kent and Hertfordshire, and the county boroughs of Croydon, East Ham and West Ham.
[2] The powers of the Minister to make regulations for controlling or regulating traffic on roads within the London Traffic Area (i.e. the area of the London and Home Counties Traffic Advisory Committee which was considerably bigger than Greater London) were contained in Section 34 and the Fourth Schedule of the Road Traffic Act, 1960.
[3] See above, Chapter III, pp. 54–58, for these regulations.

of the working party whose recommendations were endorsed by the London Boroughs Association on March 8, 1967, dealt with such topics as the supply of survey information to the London borough councils[1] and delays in the consideration of planning applications.[2]

Valuable as the discussions of the working party have been they could not resolve fundamental differences of view which also first disclosed themselves in early discussions on the content of the regulations to be made under the 1963 Act. These differences revolved round the question how much control of the planning situation the G.L.C. needed to carry out their role as a strategic authority. On planning applications, for example, it could be generally agreed that the aim should be that the G.L.C. should see all applications of major importance. But the translation of this aim into practical terms posed difficult problems. The G.L.C. sought to extend the range of applications which came to them; the boroughs claimed that to do so would mean that a great many trivial applications, which the boroughs could perfectly well deal with, would be going to the G.L.C., and would lead to delays in the whole application process.[3]

Again, on the question of the Greater London Development Plan, the G.L.C. sought to widen the scope of the regulations in order to enable more emphasis to be put on the G.L.C.'s traffic and highways responsibilities in the G.L.D.P. There has also been a good deal of dispute about the date of submission of the G.L.D.P. Originally, the Ministry had wanted this to be done within two years, that is, by April 1, 1967. The Ministry's desire for speed was echoed by the boroughs who could not go ahead with their borough plans until the G.L.D.P. had been approved. The G.L.C., however, argued for more time, pleading the complexity of the task and the need to take fully into account the results of surveys and especially the London traffic survey. On this issue the G.L.C. succeeded in convincing the Ministry and the date of submission was fixed as December 31, 1968. In the event, it became clear in 1968 that this would still not give sufficient time, and the date was postponed until July 31, 1969.[4]

Inevitably, the regulations which were issued represented a compromise between the views of the G.L.C. and the boroughs. They were, however, only a stage in the process of working out the new system. It is evident for example that the G.L.D.P. is the key to

[1] On surveys, see below, p. 102.

[2] Minutes of L.B.A. Meeting, March 8, 1967.

[3] See *Report* of G.L.C. Planning and Communications Committee, in Minutes of G.L.C. Meeting January 26, 1965; also below, p. 115.

[4] See G.L.C. Minutes, December 14, 1965, and May 21, 1968; also *Report* of L.B.A. Works Committee considered at L.B.A. Meeting, July 24, 1968.

London's long-term planning, and consequently that existing arrangements will need to be modified when the G.L.D.P. has been approved.

Thus the development control regulations[1] which laid down the categories of planning application which the boroughs were to refer to the G.L.C. either for decision or for directions were not regarded as the final word on the subject. Two years after their introduction, the Joint Working Party of G.L.C. and borough officers reviewed them. The borough's view was that since the whole question was bound up so much with the nature and form of the G.L.D.P. a review of the regulations should be deferred until the Plan had been agreed. Meanwhile, however, they put on record their view that too many trifling applications were going to the G.L.C., and that ultimately the boroughs would only need to refer applications substantially departing from the G.L.D.P. which they wished to allow. The G.L.C.'s view was that it was necessary for them to have a wider view of applications if they were effectively to ensure that the G.L.D.P. was being carried out.

THE PROBLEM OF CENTRAL LONDON

Undoubtedly, however, the present situation, in which planning has to be carried out on the basis of existing plans while a new system is being evolved, has brought many difficulties. A particular problem which was much discussed at the time of the parliamentary proceedings on the London Government Bill was the position of central London. This area including the City, the Houses of Parliament and Whitehall, contains a large part of London's outstanding buildings, and has a unique place in many aspects of the life of the capital and indeed of the country as a whole. Under the pre-1965 system its planning had been the responsibility of the L.C.C. Under the 1963 Act responsibility was split between a number of London boroughs and the City. Attempts were made in Parliament to have the planning of central London brought under the control of the G.L.C. but these were resisted by the Government on the grounds that the general provisions were sufficient to ensure that the importance of central London was not overlooked.[2]

Nevertheless, the boroughs, who must under the new system play a large part in the planning and development of the central area, have acknowledged the need for co-ordination of effort and formed

[1] The Town and Country Planning (Local Planning Authorities in Greater London) Regulations 1965 (S.I. 1965, No. 679).

[2] For a full discussion of the issues involved, see W. A. Robson, *The Heart of Greater London* (Greater London Paper No. 9, L.S.E., 1965).

a Central London Planning Conference. The members were originally the City and the boroughs of Westminster, Camden, Islington,
Southwark and Lambeth; they were later joined by Tower Hamlets
and Kensington & Chelsea. The Conference has considered such
topics as civic design and the problems of environmental areas which
overlap borough boundaries, but one of its most important tasks
so far has been to consider in detail and draw up a report on the
present and future functions of the central area. The immediate aim
was to arrive after discussion with the G.L.C. at some acceptable
statement for incorporation in the G.L.D.P., but there can be no
doubt about the necessity for special attention to the planning
problems of central London. As the history of proposals for development of some important individual parts of this area shows, it
will not be easy to reconcile all the various relevant factors in practice. Piccadilly Circus, although only one of a number of central area
redevelopment proposals, is perhaps the best-known example.
As long ago as 1959 the L.C.C. took the initiative in preparing a
scheme for an important part of the Piccadilly Circus area (the
Monico site). The Minister of Housing and Local Government took
the view that there should be a comprehensive plan for the whole
area; accordingly, the L.C.C. commissioned Lord Holford whose
report was made in March 1962. This, however, ran into the difficulty
that although, in the words of a Government working party, it
provided a 'very attractive scheme', including a large pedestrian
concourse, it did not cater for the possibility of a very large increase
of traffic.

The L.C.C., however, and Lord Holford feared that attempts to
provide for a large increase in traffic would prevent satisfactory
redevelopment of the Circus. After further discussion with the
Ministries of Housing and Local Government and Transport, the
L.C.C. agreed to take part in a joint working party consisting of
representatives of these three bodies plus Westminster and the firm
of consultants who were carrying out the London Traffic Survey.
This working party was set up in 1964 and reported in March 1965,
its main conclusion being that any scheme for the Piccadilly Circus
should use a 'double deck' approach – traffic at ground level and
pedestrians above.[1] Once again Lord Holford was invited to prepare
a scheme, but this time the invitation came from the new authorities
of the G.L.C. and the London borough of the City of Westminster.
His report went to the G.L.C. and Westminster in August 1966,
and after further lengthy discussions between the authorities, central
government departments and the private developers, a detailed scheme

[1] See 'Piccadilly Circus', *Report* of the Working Party (H.M.S.O., 1965).

was published by the G.L.C. in July 1968. This too has encountered criticisms[1] and it remains to be seen whether and when the redevelopment of Piccadilly Circus will take place.

Clearly, the new system of local government has not so far made it any easier to find a quick and effective answer to problems like Piccadilly Circus. On the one hand, the G.L.C.'s strategic role should enable it in a case like this to take a broad view of planning and traffic considerations; on the other hand, the borough (in this case the City of Westminster) now has a strong planning role and its views have considerable weight. There could be conflict between the two viewpoints. Much will turn, therefore, on how problems are resolved.[2]

GREATER LONDON DEVELOPMENT PLAN

It was suggested above that a vital stage in the evolution of the new system of London government would be the production of the G.L.D.P. One of the earliest tasks of the G.L.C. was to consult with the boroughs and the Ministry of Housing and Local Government on the all-important survey work which would be needed as a basis for the Plan. It was agreed that the three major subjects to be covered were land use, employment and housing.[3] Of these, the first was designed to show the existing uses of land and trends and changes over a period of time. It was the fundamental element in existing development plans but one immediate difficulty was that the information available varied enormously from one part of Greater London to another, both in its completeness and in its date of compilation.[4] It was therefore decided to carry out a complete survey of outer London in order to provide the latest information about land use on a uniform pattern; in inner London (the old L.C.C. area) all that was needed was to bring up to date the information which was already available. The survey has been carried out by the boroughs acting for the G.L.C.

The employment and housing surveys raised more difficulties

[1] See, for example, *The Times*, August 24, 1968, 'New Piccadilly Plan into Limbo'.

[2] An interesting development under the new system has been the formation of consortia of the G.L.C. and individual boroughs for large redevelopment schemes: the redevelopment of Covent Garden, for example, is being undertaken jointly by the G.L.C., Westminster and Camden.

[3] See report of Planning and Communications Committee in G.L.C. Minutes July 6, 1965, pp. 463–5.

[4] For example, no comprehensive survey of the parts of Greater London formerly in Kent has been carried out since 1949.

largely because these were new fields. There were, it is true, official statistics on employment but in the view of the G.L.C. these were inadequate to enable them to formulate a statement on employment policy as they were required under the Regulations relating to the G.L.D.P. They therefore concluded that they would have to carry out a survey of employment in London.[1] This was to be a complex affair involving interviews with a sample of different classes and types of employing bodies; it was undertaken by market research consultants engaged by the G.L.C.

The G.L.D.P. was to have a written statement on residential densities and the number of persons likely to be accommodated in each borough. The Milner Holland Report[2] had drawn attention to the inadequacy of data on the stock of dwellings in Greater London. From the point of view therefore of both planning and housing there was a need for further information. It was planned to obtain information, first on the useful future life of dwellings and their capacity for improvement; and, secondly, from households on their need for housing currently and in the future.

All these surveys were planned or in progress, together with the London Transportation Study (discussed below), when in November, 1966, the G.L.C. issued a Preliminary Report on the G.L.D.P. This document was largely a general statement of what needed to be done.

Towards the end of March 1969, the G.L.C. issued the draft text of the written statement for the G.L.D.P. This is an important document because for the first time it enables an assessment to be made of the role which the G.L.C. sees for itself in the production of a strategic plan for London.

The first thing to be noted about this document is its tentative nature. It makes the valid point that unlike the traditional development plan under the 1947 Act, the G.L.D.P. is not a plan for a specified number of years but rather one stage in a continuing process. But in addition it emphasises in a number of places how much planning in Greater London depends on the part played by the boroughs. Thus although the G.L.D.P. is to provide the context for the borough plans, 'the possibility must be accepted that when the borough plans are prepared within its context there will emerge considerations that call for the context to be revised'.[3] It is therefore presented as a 'conceptual plan', a 'set of ideas' for the future development of Greater London, part of a process which will require,

[1] G.L.C. Minutes June 21, 1966.

[2] *Housing in Greater London*, Cmnd. 2605 (H.M.S.O., 1965).

[3] These and other quotations are from the draft text. The statement as subsequently amended was published by the G.L.C. in September 1969.

for success, a 'sustained effort of partnership' between the G.L.C. and the boroughs.

Most of the individual sections of the report are in keeping with this approach. Thus on central London the statement says that further study is required with the boroughs to determine the functions which central London 'really should accommodate', and that the G.L.C. will co-operate with the boroughs in developing 'criteria of selectivity' to guide decisions on new uses which may be proposed.

The second main impression left by the document is that it is not so much a plan as a series of statements of view or policy on a number of different matters which often seem not to be closely related. In this it follows the letter of the Regulations[1] which set out item by item the policy statements which are required. Some sections thus cover a wide variety of topics: that on 'Town and Landscape', for example, deals, among other things, with areas of metropolitan importance (that is, with 'precincts and amenity areas which are considered by the Council to be of metropolitan importance'), with high buildings and with London squares, without really showing how policies on these topics are related to one another.

One question raised by the draft G.L.D.P. statement is whether it fulfils the intentions of the 1963 Act. As has already been stressed,[2] that Act made both the G.L.C. and the boroughs planning authorities. It did not give the G.L.C. overriding powers in the making of the development plan, except to the extent that any plans put forward by the boroughs were to be consistent with the G.L.D.P. The G.L.C. seem to have interpreted their role as being to allow the boroughs the maximum freedom in drawing up their own plans. For the most part, this means that G.L.C. statements of policy are of a very general nature – for example on London squares the Council 'declares its view that their character must be kept'; parks are classified according to size and accessibility as guides to siting and location, and it is suggested that the boroughs 'should pursue these principles and standards as a basis for a rational distribution of public open space'.

Certainly this method gives the advantage of flexibility, but does it at the same time weaken the chance of effectively planning the future of Greater London? Perhaps the most interesting part of the document is in its discussion of the basic issues of population and employment, largely concerned with the period to 1981 (chosen as being a census year). The G.L.C. expect a decline in Greater London's population amounting to between 650,000 and 870,000 between 1961

---

[1] S.I. 1966, No. 48; see above, p. 57.
[2] Above, p. 55.

and 1981, giving a total population in the latter year of 7·1 million, as a lower estimate, or 7·3 million as a higher estimate. The estimates for individual boroughs have, however, been queried by many of the boroughs concerned who have proposed higher figures: Greenwich, for example, has suggested a 1981 figure of 311,000 population against the G.L.C.'s higher estimate of 227,000, Bromley, 328,000 against 306,000. The G.L.C. have asked the boroughs to use the G.L.C. estimated populations as a basis for their plans, but have left the way open for the boroughs to demonstrate that their estimates are attainable. Again, on employment the G.L.C. see the possibility of a fall in the resident work force of 700,000 by 1981 and have declared their policy to be to try to limit this fall; they have therefore estimated net changes in industrial and office floor space as a guide to the boroughs.

Population and employment are, however, the key to much else in the planning of London's future. The difference between the G.L.C.'s higher estimate of population and the total of what the boroughs consider reasonable is considerable, amounting to 600,000 or 8 per cent. In keeping with the G.L.C.'s interpretation of its role under the 1963 Act the answers to the size and location of London's population will emerge only gradually as a result of the continuing dialogue between the G.L.C. and the boroughs. This gives great scope to the boroughs but raises doubts about the effectiveness of the new system in practice.

There is, however, one part of the draft statement which does give a more definite and specific plan of the future. This is the plan for a primary road system. It forms part of the section on Transport, which is one of the largest and most detailed sections of the whole document. The background to the production of this plan must be seen in the context of the division of powers in the highways and traffic fields under the 1963 Act, and the developments which have followed that Act.

ROADS AND TRAFFIC

The G.L.C.'s powers may be regarded as falling into several distinct categories. There are first the strategic planning powers, exemplified in the Act's provision that the G.L.D.P. is to include 'guidance as to the future road system'; and in the specific requirements of the Development Plan Regulations.[1] Then there are the regulatory powers, notably the power to make traffic regulation orders; these powers are subject to the important statutory duty on the G.L.C. to

[1] 1963 Act, Section 25(3): S.I. 1966 No. 48, Reg. 11 (e), (f), (j), (o).

consult the boroughs affected and also the police. Next are the executive powers; the G.L.C. has power, with borough consent, to provide
parking accommodation, and it is the highway authority for metropolitan roads. Finally, there are the agency functions of issuing
vehicle and driving licences.

The first category of powers is closely linked with the G.L.C.'s
role as a planning authority. The executive and regulatory powers
involve close co-operation with other bodies, notably the boroughs.
These points are discussed further below.

The Herbert Commission argued strongly the advantages of
having a single authority responsible for land use and highway
planning in Greater London. The G.L.C. is subject, under the 1963
Act, to the important limitation on its powers that trunk roads
remain the responsibility of the Ministry of Transport. It is also
important to remember that until 1968 two separate departments
and two separate committees were responsible for planning on the
one hand and highways on the other, with consequent problems of
internal co-ordination. One of the most interesting documents so far
produced by the G.L.C. is the plan for a primary road network
which was endorsed by the Council on November 21, 1967. The
essential parts of this have been incorporated in the Greater
London Development Plan.

Proposals for a comprehensive system of primary roads in London
have a long history. In recent years the need has been felt for up-to-
date information about the amount and type of traffic using the
streets of London as a preliminary to drawing up plans for the
future. Following a suggestion of the Nugent Committee[1] the L.C.C.
and the Ministry of Transport commissioned a London Traffic
Survey in 1961. This covered the Greater London conurbation; it
consisted of 50,000 household interviews carried out in 1962 with
questions on such things as car ownership and travel habits, together
with roadside interviews and traffic counts. The results were published in 1964 by the L.C.C. as Volume 1 of the Survey.

The second stage of the Survey was an attempt to define the extent
and nature of travel patterns in London as they were likely to be by
1971 and 1981, including an estimate of the number of vehicles
using the road network. The results of this were published in 1966
by the G.L.C. as Volume II of the Survey.

The G.L.C. decided in 1965 that in order to prepare its transport
plan for the G.L.D.P. a third stage was necessary. This third stage,
named the London Transportation Study, aimed to use the data from

[1] *Report* of Inter-departmental Committee on London Roads (H.M.S.O.,
1959).

the first and second stages to evaluate a large number of alternative transport plans. It was originally hoped to complete this by September 1967, and to use the results as available for the G.L.D.P. work, but this proved too optimistic a time-table. Nevertheless, it was claimed by the head of the Policy and Research Branch of the G.L.C.'s Department of Highways and Transportation: 'it is believed that the work to be undertaken will represent one of the most complete analyses ever made of transport proposals for a city region'.[1]

It is against this background of continuing analysis and evaluation of London's transport needs generally that one must set the plan for the primary road network. The most striking feature of the proposals[2] and the one which has aroused most controversy is the suggestion for a motorway box, that is, a ring road encircling inner London to be built as an urban motorway. Apart from this, the primary road network would consist of two further ring roads, the outer one of which would lie partly outside Greater London. It was estimated that, over the period 1971–83, £650 million would be required for these primary roads; and with secondary roads added the total would be £860 million.

The idea of a high-capacity road to carry motor traffic round inner London was not new. But the G.L.C.'s decision of November 1967 was the first time that there had been a commitment to a definite plan by a body exercising authority and commanding resources over a sufficiently wide area to make it feasible that the plan could be carried out. Whether it will be carried out on the scale and in the time hoped for by the G.L.C. remains to be seen. Already a London Motorway Action Group has been formed under the chairmanship of Mr Douglas Jay to oppose these proposals on the grounds of their enormous cost, and the damage and upheaval they would cause to housing and the environment generally.[3]

The close links between road planning and land-use planning have been recognised in the reorganisation of the G.L.C. committee structure carried out in 1968. Before then, rather cumbersome arrangements for joint committees and sub-committees of the Highways and Traffic Committee and the Planning and Communications Committee had to be devised to consider important matters such as

---

[1] Brian Martin: 'London Transportation Study' (*Quarterly Bulletin*, G.L.C. Research & Intelligence Unit, No. 1, Dec. 1967, pp. 19–20.

[2] *London's Roads – The Council's Objective* (G.L.C., November 1967).

[3] See 'Cars, Cities and the Box' by Douglas Jay (*Guardian*, August 12, 1968). The Labour Opposition on the G.L.C. also seemed to have doubts about the motorway box by the time the draft G.L.D.P. was published in March 1969.

the road proposals. These are now dealt with by the Strategic Planning Committee.

Traffic management

Traffic management brings the G.L.C. more closely into contact with the boroughs and also with the police. It is now the responsibility of the Planning and Transportation Committee, acting through four area committees (Central London, North-East, South and West). Major schemes for traffic management are put forward by the G.L.C. and approved after consultation with the boroughs, the police, and other interested parties. Minor schemes, which generally involve no more than waiting restrictions or one-way working in a particular street, are proposed by the boroughs or the police. Major schemes may involve a whole series of one-way workings, prohibition of turns and new traffic lights.

There has been a marked increase in the number of orders made by the G.L.C. bringing traffic schemes into effect, from 92 in 1965–6 to 255 in 1966–7 and 352 in 1967–8. Many of these schemes were, however, planned by the London Traffic Management Unit of the Ministry of Transport whose powers the G.L.C. inherited.

Apart from traffic management schemes, and related activities such as the urban clearway programme of the G.L.C. – of which over 200 miles had been brought into operation by the middle of 1968 – parking policy is an important element in the powers which the London authorities possess to deal with the traffic problem. The G.L.C. is responsible for Orders and Regulations governing controlled parking zones in London; and both the G.L.C. and the boroughs have power to provide off-street parking. Over and above this the G.L.C. is required to provide in the G.L.D.P. 'a statement of policy as to the provision of public and private car parks throughout Greater London'.[1]

A preliminary statement on parking policy was approved by the G.L.C. on February 22, 1966, based largely on existing policies; it included a proposal to extend the controlled parking area in central London from its existing 8 square miles to 40 square miles covering the whole or part of eleven boroughs and the City (the Inner London Parking Area). A more extended statement for inclusion in the G.L.D.P. after discussion with the boroughs was approved on May 7, 1968; among other things it suggested discussions with borough councils of a programme for providing off-street public car parks, as well as an extension of on-street parking.

[1] Town and Country Planning (Development Plans for Greater London) Regulations, 1966, Reg. 11(o). For recent proposed changes, see below, p. 113.

There is obviously a need for close co-operation between the G.L.C. and the boroughs if the division of powers laid down in the 1963 Act is to work effectively. At the same time it must be recognised that there are bound to be conflicts of view, where for example traffic needs come into conflict with local amenity. The borough argument was set out in their evidence to the Redcliffe-Maud Commission; they claimed that there were delays in reaching decisions over traffic management schemes, and a loss of local initiative. 'There is also a tendency on the part of the Greater London Council to give greater weight to the solution of traffic management problems than to the preservation of a good standard of residential environment.'[1] To the G.L.C. on the other hand the situation appeared rather differently:

'There is still, however, no single authority responsible for traffic management, since the police retain separate but overlapping functions; the Minister of Transport has certain traffic management responsibilities; and the London borough councils have functions in respect of car-parking schemes.'[2]

The important point is that to some extent both the boroughs and the G.L.C. may be right; but the new system will be judged on whether it is seen to be making an effective contribution towards solving London's traffic problems without subordinating every other consideration to this aim. One can easily cite cases where there have been difficulties and delays arising from conflicts of view. A proposal for controlled parking in the Kensington High Street area in 1967, for example, aroused such strong local protests that the Borough of Kensington & Chelsea proposed a new scheme. Again, a proposed traffic management scheme for Cricklewood Broadway, which was agreed in principle by the G.L.C. in December 1965, was not finally agreed until after prolonged discussions with the boroughs concerned and the Ministry of Transport in April 1967.[3] Cases like this induced the G.L.C. to press for greater powers and the outcome of this approach is discussed below.

Roads

Before looking at these later developments, however, the position in the highways field must be examined. Here, too, the Act laid down a division of responsibilities, but this time a division into three. The

[1] London Boroughs Association: Statement of Evidence to the Royal Commission on Local Government in England, October 1966, para. 34.

[2] G.L.C. Minutes, November 15, 1966, p. 617.

[2] ibid. February 13, 1968, Questions.

Ministry of Transport retained responsibility for the 150 miles of trunk roads in Greater London, the G.L.C. for 550 miles of metro-politan roads[1] and the boroughs for the remaining 7,000 miles of roads. The main responsibilities were for construction, maintenance, and lighting.

Metropolitan roads were a new category; the intention was to include in it those roads which served as through routes. These were largely but not entirely Class I roads according to the Ministry's classification for grant purposes as it then was. The Class I roads in the metropolitan roads category comprised 60 per cent of the total mileage of such roads in Greater London. However, in 1967 the Ministry revised the basis of its classification for grant purposes into 'principal' and 'other' roads, the former qualifying for 75 per cent grant as being essential traffic routes in the national system. All the metropolitan roads and 325 miles of borough roads were classified as principal roads. It should be noted that this classification does not correspond to the categories used by the G.L.C. and the Ministry in planning the road network, where major roads (corresponding to trunk and principal roads) are sub-divided into primary and secondary roads.

In practice, the confusion over classification and terminology has not led to any difficulty in the day-to-day activities of maintenance which are carried out by the boroughs; for metropolitan roads they act under delegated powers from the G.L.C. Similarly, the G.L.C. has retained control over policy and design for street lighting in metropolitan roads but has delegated the work of installation and maintenance to the boroughs.[2]

Partly, however, because of the lack of defined criteria which lies behind the confusion over classification, there has been some argument over the extent of metropolitan roads. In October 1966 the London Boroughs Association told the Royal Commission on Local Government in England that they 'should only be the really major traffic routes' and reported that they were considering a suggestion that the mileage of metropolitan roads should be reduced by about 50 per cent.[3] This point should be easily met by using data from the London Traffic Survey which was not available when the London Government Act was framed. The boroughs' attitude was not, however, governed entirely by the desire to have control over as

[1] Originally there were about 530 miles of metropolitan roads specified in the 1963 Act, but a number of adjustments were agreed with the boroughs in 1964–5.

[2] G.L.C. Minutes, December 14, 1965, pp. 843–4.

[3] Statement of Evidence, para. 33.

large a part of the road system as possible. Under the Regulations
relating to planning applications, the boroughs were required to
submit to the G.L.C. all applications for development within 220 feet
of the centre of a metropolitan road.[1] Although the intention behind
this was clearly to give the G.L.C. control over developments
which could seriously affect their traffic and highway responsibilities
the boroughs saw it as meaning that a large number of trivial applications had to be sent to the G.L.C. with consequent delays. Moreover, in certain areas of central London the network of metropolitan roads was so dense that this requirement covered quite a
high proportion of all applications in these areas.

PROPOSALS FOR CHANGE

A number of factors combined to bring about changes in the system
established by the 1963 Act. First, the G.L.C. increasingly felt
that it was being hampered in its efforts to deal with the traffic
situation by lack of adequate powers. Secondly, an important element in transport planning, public transport, had been left unaffected
by the 1963 Act. Thirdly, under an energetic new Minister of Transport, Mrs Barbara Castle, the Ministry of Transport showed itself
ready to make changes in its own powers during 1966 and 1967.
Fourthly, the Conservatives who won control of the G.L.C. in 1967
had pledged themselves to deal more vigorously with London's
traffic problems. The outcome of lengthy discussion between the
various parties concerned was the publication of a White Paper in
July 1968.[2]

In December 1966 the G.L.C. resolved that 'subject to the formu-
lation of satisfactory administrative and financial arrangements'
it was prepared to play a leading role in establishing a transport
authority in London, with the particular implication that it would in
so doing be directly involved in the policies and finances of the
London Transport Board. The Council felt that this was a logical
step for it to take as the policy-making body for transportation
generally in London.[3] The immediate occasion was the discussion of
a Government White Paper which among other things proposed the
establishment of transport authorities in certain conurbations in
the provinces to be responsible for the running of public transport
in these areas.[4] In London the particular problems of the London

[1] S.I. 1965, No. 679, Reg. 4(f).
[2] *Transport in London* (Cmnd. 3686, H.M.S.O., 1968).
[3] G.L.C. Minutes, December 13, 1966, pp. 710–13.
[4] *Transport Policy* (Cmnd. 3057, H.M.S.O., 1966).

Transport Board were to be the subject of a special review.[1]

Apart from informal contacts, the only medium through which the G.L.C. could discuss transport problems of mutual interest at that time was the Transport Co-ordinating Council for London (T.C.C.L.). This was set up by the Minister in March 1966 with representatives of the ministry, G.L.C., L.T.B., B.R. and the boroughs. But as its name implies, this body could only attempt to co-ordinate under the chairmanship of the Minister, the plans of a number of diverse and independent authorities, and this was not in the G.L.C.'s view the ideal arrangement.

Clearly, a close association between the G.L.C. and L.T.B., whatever form it took, was a major issue which would require considerable discussion and negotiation. Before much progress had been made, the possibility was raised of widening these discussions. During the election campaign preceding the G.L.C. elections in April 1967, the Conservatives argued that the G.L.C. needed increased powers in the highways and traffic fields and proposed if they were elected a 'package deal' with the boroughs under which the G.L.C. would surrender some powers in planning, housing, licensing and parks and open spaces in return for some of the boroughs' powers in highways and traffic. Negotiations were opened with the L.B.A. shortly after the Conservatives were returned to power.[2] But some of the increased powers wanted by the G.L.C. belonged to the Ministry of Transport, and that department would in any case need to be consulted particularly as legislation would be needed for most of what the G.L.C. were proposing. Fortunately, the Ministry quite independently were coming round to the view that 'the powers of local authorities in relation to transport and traffic matters must be improved.'[3] Circumstances were therefore favourable to the G.L.C.'s approach at this time not only on the larger question of London Transport, but also on the smaller yet still very important question of the strengthening of existing powers of the G.L.C. On December 15, 1967, it was announced that agreement had been reached between the Minister (Mrs Barbara Castle) and the Leader of the G.L.C. (Mr Desmond Plummer) on the principles of a major reorganisation of the G.L.C.'s responsibilities. The details are embodied in the White Paper of July 1968.[4]

The fundamental purpose of the proposals in the White Paper

[1] On this and London Transport generally see pp. 158–165.

[2] See G.L.C. Minutes, June 20, 1967.

[3] White Paper *Public Transport and Traffic* (Cmnd. 3481, H.M.S.O., 1967), para. 113.

[4] The Transport (London) Act, 1969, gives effect to the White Paper proposals.

was to give the G.L.C. the powers to enable it to integrate planning, major highway functions, traffic measures and the broad direction of passenger transport services. The White Paper listed the main defects in the existing arrangements as (i) lack of a single body responsible for planning transport in London; (ii) lack of co-ordination between the providers of public transport and those who determine the traffic and pricing environment; (iii) 'in many respects' transport planning is 'at arm's length' from land-use planning.[1]

To remedy the situation the following measures were proposed:

(a) G.L.C. to be the transport planning authority with the duty of preparing and publishing Transport Plans (dealing for example with long-term investment proposals);

(b) G.L.C. to be responsible for appointing a London Transport Executive to run passenger transport services; G.L.C. to control general policies, budgets and fares policy;

(c) G.L.C. to have a closer financial relationship with British Rail and particularly to be consulted about fares proposals;

(d) G.L.C. to become highway authority for all principal roads, and ultimately of trunk roads as well, with some modification in the arrangements for development control;[2]

(e) G.L.C.'s powers to be strengthened in relation to on-street parking, installing traffic signals, imposing speed limits, and to be augmented, e.g. by including control over bus stops and routes;

(f) a joint Traffic Executive to be set up between the G.L.C. and the Metropolitan Police.

January 1, 1970 has been fixed for the transfer of responsibility of London Transport to the G.L.C. The latter have throughout the negotiations argued that before taking over London Transport they must be sure that the undertaking is financially viable, and earning at the time of transfer a surplus sufficient to create a reserve to meet contingencies. The White Paper specified some of the measures proposed by the Government to help London Transport meet this condition.[3] It remained nevertheless the point of most difficulty in the final negotiations. The G.L.C. argued that since in future any deficit on London Transport's working would have to be met by the

[1] Cmnd. 3686, paras, 33–5.
[2] There will be two classes of application for development: (i) as at present; (ii) those which the boroughs will be able to determine 'subject to their operating . . . within a framework indicated to them by the G.L.C. from time to time after consultation' (ibid, para. 60).
[3] See below, p. 164.

H

ratepayers of Greater London, it was right that they should at least start with a clean sheet.[1]

CONCLUSION

The publication of the White Paper on Transport in London was a tacit acknowledgment that the changes introduced by the 1963 Act were not sufficient to create an authority capable of dealing effectively with London's traffic and transport problems. In large part this can be traced back to the fact that public transport was excluded from the terms of reference of the Herbert Commission. It was also true no doubt that the immense political struggle which preceded the introduction of the new system of local government in Greater London left little time for the consideration of changes involving not only local government but also the nationalised transport industry. Nevertheless, it is an interesting commentary on London's problems that scarcely three years after the new system came into effect such a major change in the scale and range of the G.L.C.'s responsibilities should be proposed.

If one asks whether the arrangements now proposed are adequate for the task of dealing with London's huge traffic and transport problem, the answer must surely be that the G.L.C. will certainly have sufficient powers to deal with the problem, so far as it can be regarded as a problem within the boundaries of Greater London.[2] One must now wait to see what use is made of those powers. A particularly important point will be the extent to which a balance is struck between the needs of transport and the wider planning considerations which the G.L.C. as the strategic planning authority for Greater London should have in mind. It would be unfortunate if the new emphasis on traffic and transport were to dominate the G.L.C.'s thinking to the detriment of those environmental considerations which are the essence of good planning. Even before the new proposals were announced there was some evidence of a 'transportation' bias, for example, in the Preliminary Report on the Greater London Development Plan of October 1966, and in the prominence which has been given to the plans for a primary road network.[3]

[1] See report of press conference on the publication of the White Paper (*The Times*, July 3, 1968).

[2] On the problems of the relation between Greater London and the rest of the South East Region, see below, Chapter VIII. An important limitation in the G.L.C.'s powers is that it will still have no effective control over the suburban railway services provided by British Rail.

[3] The draft statement of the G.L.D.P. gives prominence to the road plan, primarily perhaps because this is a sphere where the G.L.C. has executive responsibility.

On the other hand, the changes in the G.L.C.'s committee structure which were announced in July 1968 should help to promote a balanced consideration of land use, traffic and communications in the long term through the Strategic Planning Committee. At the same time, it must be remembered that until 1969 there were two separate departments each under a chief officer responsible for planning on the one hand and traffic and highways on the other. These departments had different and to some extent conflicting aims, a situation which can sometimes lead to one department's succeeding in pressing its views at the expense of the other. These are potential dangers. They must be set against the undoubted fact that under the system brought in by the 1963 Act as modified by the legislation following the 1968 White Paper, there is now for the first time a single body with the powers and the capacity to plan for the needs of Greater London in terms of physical development and transport.

Two interrelated questions now arise; how effective are the arrangements for carrying out such plans; and what is the position of the boroughs? So far as traffic and transport are concerned, the strengthened powers of the G.L.C. mean that it can effectively carry out its plans, subject of course to the ultimate restraint exercised over any local authority by the central government. But conversely, it appears that the White Paper gives the boroughs a diminished role in these fields. In the arrangements for preparation of development plans and for development control the position seems to be less clear cut.

The division of powers in the 1963 Act between the G.L.C. and the boroughs was intended to represent a division of interests. It was explicitly stated by the Government in the course of proceedings on the Bill that there was no question of making the G.L.C. a superior authority to the boroughs, but simply of its having wider responsibilities. On this basis, the boroughs would have two concerns in the questions discussed in this chapter. First, they should have responsibility for matters which are purely or very largely of local concern; in this would clearly be included responsibility for the many miles of roads and streets which are of only local significance; also included would be the large number of minor planning applications (e.g. by a householder wishing to erect a garage) which form the bulk of applications going to local authorities. Secondly, they would expect at least to be able to voice their views on strategic issues which had a direct effect on their own areas, and perhaps to have some degree of influence on the decisions taken.

The latter point is the one which gives rise to the most difficulty in practice. In the nature of the situation there are bound to be occasions when a decision on a strategic issue will profoundly affect borough interests. The line of the motorway box is an obvious big issue of this kind. But traffic schemes which seem obviously sensible to the G.L.C. may well conflict with the boroughs' ideas of what kind of environment they want to see in their areas. There is also the other side of the picture. What the borough may see as desirable and entirely reasonable for the planning of their own area may well conflict with what the G.L.C. is trying to do in planning for London as a whole. This seems to be leading to a situation where the G.L.C. increasingly leaves questions of amenity and environment to be raised by the boroughs.

It is obviously right that, as the Act provides, there should be consultation and discussion between the G.L.C. and the boroughs over these questions. The danger is that apart from delaying decisions which may be a necessary price to pay for ensuring that legitimate interests are heard, the result may be a compromise which fails in both directions, neither effectively ensuring a proper plan for Greater London nor enabling the boroughs to create the kind of life and environment which they desire. The danger arises particularly because of the size of the boroughs; and it is essentially a question of planning.

The boroughs are large and powerful authorities, much larger and more powerful than had been recommended by the Herbert Commission. The consequence is twofold. Many of them, such as Camden and Westminster, have been enabled to set up large and efficient planning departments which are very much alive to London's planning problems but naturally look at them through their own borough's eyes. Secondly, the G.L.C. has generally shown itself anxious to be accommodating to the boroughs' point of view in a way which might not have been so evident if the boroughs had been more numerous and less strong. These tendencies have been reinforced by the L.B.A.'s ability to speak strongly on behalf of the boroughs as a whole.

The effects are hard to assess at this stage, but the one thing which can certainly be said is that the success of the planning arrangements under the 1963 Act depends on an exceedingly delicate balance of powers between the G.L.C. and the boroughs which has yet to prove itself.

Chapter VI

LONDON BOROUGH SERVICES

In this chapter we deal mainly with those services which the London boroughs inherited from the former counties and county boroughs, and, especially, the personal health, welfare and children's services, which (together with education in the outer boroughs) provided one of the most controversial elements in the arrangements for the transfer of functions under the new system.

Any attempt to assess the effect of the reforms on these services is faced with a number of difficulties. First, the new system has only been in operation a short time, and many of the advantages which might be expected to accrue are in *posse* rather than in *esse*. Secondly, general changes unconnected with the London reforms have been taking place in these services, as in the children's service with the coming into operation of the Children and Young Persons Act, 1963. Thirdly, there is not much published information available, and what there is at the time of writing relates at latest to the year ending March 31, 1967. Borough councils are under no obligation to produce general annual reports on their work, and to the best of our knowledge only one, Bromley, has done so. There are, however, statutory annual reports of Medical Officers of Health, sometimes including information on welfare and children's services; in addition, some boroughs produce annual reports on the children's service and at least one (Southwark) has prepared a report on the welfare services in the borough.

In the following account, much use is made of information drawn from the annual reports of the Medical Officers of Health. In addition, on the statistical side, there are the annual Health, Welfare and Children's Statistics published by the Institute of Municipal Treasurers and Accountants; the three Ministry of Health publications, *Health and Welfare – the Development of Community Care*, enable some comparisons to be made between the provisions and plans of the pre-1965 authorities and those of the new London boroughs.

In general, a study of the reports of the Medical Officers of Health of the London boroughs leaves three predominating impressions. First, that the transfer was effected with remarkable smoothness: the general public hardly seems to have noticed that any change was taking place. Secondly, a notable degree of co-operation and co-ordinated effort appears to have been achieved between departments within boroughs, between boroughs and between the official services and voluntary effort. Thirdly, there is an enthusiasm and expectancy in many reports which indicate a consciousness of a challenge, and an eagerness to respond to it.

CO-ORDINATION AND CO-OPERATION

As the Seebohm Committee have indicated,[1] the London boroughs have made a variety of arrangements for dealing with their health and welfare responsibilities. Thus although seventeen have separate welfare committees to which a chief welfare officer is responsible, five have a joint health and welfare committee to which a chief welfare officer is responsible, two have a welfare committee to which a Medical Officer of Health is responsible, and the remaining eight a joint health and welfare committee to which a Medical Officer of Health is responsible. In one borough (Harrow) the health, welfare and children's services are united in one department, although there is a separate children's committee, as is required by statute.

The Seebohm report stressed the indivisibility of the welfare services and the Ministry of Health Green Paper of 1968[2] stressed that of the National Health Service. In the light of these documents, it is interesting to note the efforts which have already been made in the London boroughs to secure a measure of integration of all the fragmented empires which have grown up as a result of past legislation. As indicated above, there are ten boroughs where the M.O.H. is responsible for welfare, one of these being Harrow where there is a combined social services department.[3] Generally in these cases, there is also a chief welfare officer; it is noteworthy that the report of the M.O.H. of Redbridge, another of the ten, emphasises that the chief welfare officer works *with* him, rather than *under* him, and has 'almost complete professional freedom'.

On the other side, in Hounslow, where there are separate health and welfare committees and chief officers, the chief welfare officer in a section which he had been invited to contribute to the M.O.H.'s

[1] *Report* of the Committee on Local Authority and Allied Personal Social Services, Cmnd. 3703 (H.M.S.O., 1968), Appendix 11.

[2] The Administrative Structure of the N.H.S. Medical and Related Services.

[3] It must be stressed that this is a field where changes are likely in a number of boroughs as the Seebohm proposals are examined.

report, writes: 'Development of the Welfare Services runs closely in parallel with the development of the Personal Health Services. It is very gratifying to record the wholehearted sense of working together which exists between the staffs of the two departments to the advantage of those in need of either service in the borough.'

A variety of other means of securing co-ordination of departmental working is to be found in the various boroughs, through committees of members and of officers. Perhaps the most far-seeing expression of the need for co-ordinated effort is to be found in Waltham Forest, where the planning officer, in a report on 'Population and Housing', emphasises the need for health and welfare to work closely with planning, housing, education and other departments 'in the evolution of gracious urban living, with provision for groups of the population with social needs integrated into it in the proportion appropriate to modern conceptions of civilization'.

Hackney has a Family Services Advisory Committee, supported by an officer's co-ordinating committee. Camden also has a Family Services Committee (without executive functions – it reports to the executive committees for action and there are regular meetings of the chief officers concerned), and is associated with London University in a research scheme on the co-ordinated planning of the social services.

In Westminster there is an officers' co-ordinating committee for the health, welfare and children's services, and also housing, with representatives from the Inner London Education Committee and the Greater London Council Housing Committee. It is assisted by a working party and a case conference.

Southwark has a similar arrangement, with a policy committee meeting quarterly, a working sub-committee and case conferences.

In Bromley, a co-ordinating Secretary for Social Services co-ordinates visits by social workers, arranges case conferences and meetings of an officer's liaison committee and organises records. Redbridge is considering the appointment of a joint training officer for all the social service departments.

In Hillingdon, co-ordination of all the departments has been a particular concern of the town clerk, with an assistant town clerk for social services under him.

Westminster and Camden are both fortunate in having been able to house their health, welfare, children's and housing departments together in modern buildings – perhaps the most certain method of securing co-ordinated effort. Most of the other boroughs are handicapped by the necessity to continue using the scattered premises passed over to them by their predecessors.

Side by side with this co-ordination of effort within the boroughs, there is a notable degree of co-operation between them, particularly in the provision of night and weekend emergency services. Joint arrangements for this purpose are made, for example, by Hackney and Islington; Wandsworth, Southwark and Lambeth; Lewisham and Greenwich; Westminster and Kensington & Chelsea.

Westminster, Kensington & Chelsea and Camden unite to meet the transport needs of the physically handicapped in their areas; Southwark and Lambeth to provide an incontinent laundry service; Harrow and Brent share the services of a medical social worker to care for the unmarried mother, as do Hillingdon, Ealing and Hounslow. Hillingdon is also associated with Hounslow and Richmond upon Thames in the West Middlesex Adoption Society which undertakes the adoption work of the children's departments in the three boroughs. These and other examples which could be quoted need to be set, however, against the difficulties which have arisen over certain arrangements. Many of the residential establishments which the boroughs inherited are shared between two or more boroughs, and this does create problems for example over staffing – problems, however, which should disappear when, as is gradually happening, all boroughs have their institutions under their own control.

All boroughs make use of the services of voluntary organisations. As the Medical Officer of Health of Waltham Forest has said: 'a very large number of activities, whose mainsprings come from sources independent of the local authority, are providing meaning to the lives of those involved, and are as fundamental an expression of the community as is the Council itself. . . . It is not only that there is a role for both statutory and voluntary effort in the social field. There is far too much work even for both put together.' And he goes on to give a list of twenty-eight organisations financially assisted by the Council, adding that there are also several important organisations not receiving grants, and very many smaller associations and clubs who play a most valuable role in social welfare.

Again, there are problems under the new system as well as advantages. The Medical Officer of Health of Barnet, acknowledging the 'inestimable contribution' of voluntary organisations, has commented 'A few of the organisations decided it would make for easier and closer links with Health and Welfare if their own area of administration coincided with the borough boundaries. Experience proved this to be of distinct value to all concerned.' But for some London-wide or national organisations, such as the National Council for the Unmarried Mother and her Child, the new system has brought serious problems; whereas previously those in the County of London could get financial support from one source, the L.C.C., there is now some difficulty in getting the boroughs to agree how much support each should give. This problem is being actively considered by the London Boroughs' Association.

One of the most effective means of co-ordination has been evolved in the welfare department of Southwark, where four social workers have been appointed and seconded to social work settlements, their functions being:

To deal with social problems arising from the contact;
To organise, train and guide groups of volunteers in association with settlements;
To organise tasks for the groups, and check their completion;
To keep the department informed of any special needs of the old and handicapped beyond the resources of the group;
To submit periodic reports both to the settlement and the department.

If it is clear that there is a general effort being made to secure that co-ordination of the welfare services which it is the aim of the recommendations of the Seebohm Committee to achieve, it is also true that much attention is being paid by the borough health authorities to the need to secure closer co-operation with the other two branches of the Health Service. More than one borough M.O.H. makes reference to the Porritt Report[1] which may be said to have fathered the Ministry of Health's Green Paper.

Though not yet organised in all boroughs, often on account of staff shortages, attachment of health visitors to group practices in particular is steadily increasing, though attachment to one man practices usually presents difficulties. Thus in Waltham Forest health visitors attend weekly clinics and discussions at nineteen surgeries, while in Bromley there are ten such attachments.

In Greenwich, on the other hand, general practitioners help to man the Council's clinics, and are also appointed as visiting medical officers. Camden issues a fortnightly bulletin, primarily for the benefit of general practitioners, but also for the staff of local hospitals, to keep them up to date regarding the services of the Council, and this now has a circulation of 1,000 copies per issue. The Mayor of Wandsworth has held a reception for the general practitioners of the borough.

Evidence of the establishment of closer relations with the hospital

[1] *A Review of the Medical Service in Great Britain* (Medical Services Review Committee, B.M.A., 1964).

service comes from a number of boroughs. In Redbridge, a health visitor goes to the local geriatric hospital weekly to ensure that necessary services are available to patients on discharge. Similar visits are paid at Hillingdon by a home nurse to the geriatric department twice weekly, and by the superintendent home nurse to the departmental sisters to find out the needs of other patients. In Greenwich, the consultant geriatrician at the local general hospital is also a part-time member of the borough medical staff. Similarly in Camden the consultant psychiatrist at the mental hospital with Camden in its catchment area has been appointed adviser in mental health to the borough.

Finally, in any attempt to secure a co-ordinated health and welfare service, it is of the utmost importance to secure the understanding and co-operation of the general public. One means by which this can be achieved is through Health Education which in the view of the M.O.H. of Hammersmith 'is perhaps the most important duty of all the officers of any health and welfare service'.

All boroughs carry out this duty, and the majority of them, following the recommendations of the Cohen Committee,[1] have appointed health education officers, and sometimes assistant health education officers too. They do so by means of exhibitions, posters, pamphlets, talks, discussion groups, film shows and playlets. Tower Hamlets records that during 1967 talks and discussion groups were arranged on 1,588 occasions with over 14,000 participants. The subjects dealt with comprised smoking and lung cancer, sex education and venereal disease, mothercraft, cervical cytology, needs of the elderly, home accidents, general health subjects, psychoprophylaxis and health education techniques. Films or film-strips were shown on 281 of these occasions.

Many boroughs have a monthly programme of topics – e.g. prevention and spread of coughs and colds in January, safety measures on holiday in July, safe toys in December. The audiences comprise school children, old people in their clubs, and other adults contacted through various voluntary organisations and through the borough's own clinics. Thus in Lewisham there are mothers' clubs and in both Lewisham and Sutton parentcraft classes, Sutton's with an average attendance of fifty. Harrow has a parent/teacher association connected with its Junior Training Centre for the mentally handicapped. Croydon has evolved a community health course of a dozen sessions for secondary schools, which is now being nationally used.

[1] *Report* of Joint Committee of the Central and Scottish Health Councils on Health Education (1964).

Many boroughs have town shows and carnivals, and a health exhibition is often a feature of these. An example of the ingenuity displayed in putting across health propaganda comes from Greenwich, where in a sideshow visitors were invited to fire suction darts at a revolving target featuring home safety questions. On registering a hit on a question the participant was invited to answer the question. A correct answer won a home safety pencil, and over a thousand pencils were thus distributed.

Apart from promoting health education, the boroughs make a wide distribution of booklets indicating the services they provide, and showing how and where they can be obtained.

The foregoing pages give examples, by no means exhaustive, of the efforts being made by the London boroughs to provide a co-ordinated health and welfare service. Many further examples could also be given of new initiatives, and new approaches to old problems.

Training

One of the greatest difficulties which faced the new boroughs especially in the welfare services, owing to the increase in the number of responsible authorities, was shortage of staff. To meet this situation they embarked on training schemes on a scale unheard of by most of the former authorities (Essex County Council being a notable exception).

Such training takes three main forms – release of staff to secure professional qualifications, generally by means of two-year courses; release for shorter periods to participate in courses run by the London Boroughs' Training Committee;[1] in-service training. Perhaps the most striking example of the last is to be found in Enfield where some thirty school leavers were appointed as supernumerary officers, and given the opportunity of working for several weeks in each of the departments of the Council. From these trainees the health department recruited six young people, already making headway in the sections in which they were placed. In Waltham Forest a Social Work Adviser has been appointed to promote and supervise training, and in many boroughs social work and field work instructors have been appointed.

One particular problem of training schemes is that an officer expensively trained by one authority may elect when qualified to transfer to another which perhaps has no such scheme. Boroughs, such as Tower Hamlets which are active in training in order to attract recruits to an unattractive area, suffer particularly in this respect.

[1] See above, p. 85.

The London Boroughs Association has made some effort to deal with this situation.

HEALTH SERVICES

Health centres were first definitely proposed by a B.M.A. Committee in 1920, but did not appear on the Statute Book until 1946, when the National Health Service Act laid upon local authorities the duty to provide, equip and maintain them. Very few authorities did so, and where they were provided they did not catch on. One of the basic ideas of the health centre was that it should provide a focus for the work of the general practitioners, but these were unwilling to rent consulting rooms in them as the rents were considered too high.

With the Ministry's Charter for General Practice, which made provision for partial reimbursement of practice premises expenditure, and also because there was a growing recognition among family doctors that the future lay with the group practice, the whole position changed in 1966, and the idea of the health centre once more came to the fore.

Two of the London boroughs – Hackney and Southwark – inherited health centres from the London County Council, the former being the John Scott centre, the first to be purpose built and the best known, and the latter the Peckham Health Centre which started as a voluntary effort.

Hounslow and Waltham Forest were first in the field with the provision of new centres. Hounslow's, which was planned in 1964, before the borough assumed its new functions, being of particular interest. Not only does it provide accommodation for general practitioners, but it also houses the head offices of the children's and welfare departments, includes a child psychiatric unit and a mental health day centre, and actually adjoins the local hospital. Four other health centres are being actively promoted in the borough.

Waltham Forest's first centre, which is purpose built, was opened in June 1966. Originally designed by the Walthamstow Borough Council, its plans were modified to accord with the additional responsibilities of the new borough to incorporate 'three medical consulting rooms with examination rooms, four dental surgeries with a dental laboratory and X-ray facilities, a four-cubicle chiropody suite, a large room for a physiotherapy unit and lecture hall, a child guidance unit, minor ailments treatment room, speech therapy unit, an acoustically treated room for testing children's hearing, waiting areas and reception offices'. Health visitors and district nurses are attached to the centre, certain hospital specialist services are provided there, and during the evening the premises are made available to voluntary organisations assisting in the health and welfare field.

Home helps and home nursing. More than one Medical Officer of Health emphasises the great importance of the home help in forestalling the need for medical and hospital treatment. Nearly all point to an increase in the use of the service, but also to the difficulties in securing recruitment. Special recruitment drives have been made in some boroughs, with considerable success, but more interesting are the efforts to raise the status of the calling.

Croydon, for example, has inaugurated, in specially adapted premises, a home help service training scheme, designed to cover all the practical work of home helps, with talks and demonstrations by professional staff, emphasising their role in supporting other workers in the domiciliary health and welfare field. An appropriate certificate is awarded on the judgment of an external examiner.

Other authorities are already operating or are planning similar training schemes. In Southwark, specially trained home helps deal with problem families. In Sutton, selected home helps, with the assistance of public health inspectors, deal with dirty homes.

The majority of boroughs have initiated 'neighbourly help' schemes, which in essence means the permanent attachment of one home help to one or two particularly handicapped cases only, to which they give continuing supervision. Thus in Camden there were sixty-five such 'good neighbours' looking after 111 clients, mostly old people. Most boroughs also operate night attendant services, but the demand is generally small.

Barking undertook a survey of all its home help cases by the senior home help organiser and a senior medical officer to assess any need of dental or ophthalmic treatment, district nurse or other service.

The home help service is today mainly concerned with assistance to the aged. The aged have benefited from the reorganisation also in the greatly increased provision of geriatric clinics, which have clearly demonstrated the part they can play in preventing senile degeneration. Hardly any of these existed before 1965, but they are now to be found in Hackney, Harrow, Greenwich, Richmond upon Thames, Brent, Barnet (where there are four), and Sutton, while in the health centre at Harrow, there is an old people's club as well as a geriatric clinic.

Medical Officers of Health do not report the same trouble in recruiting 'home nurses' as some other grades of staff, but a difficulty here has been that much of their time has been spent on tasks for which their skills are not required. Accordingly, a number of boroughs are now employing nursing auxiliaries and bathing assistants, while Waltham Forest has a team of this kind operating from the welfare department.

Home nurses as well as health visitors are in some boroughs attached to general practitioners. The chief obstacle to this is the scattered nature of some practices. In the view of the Medical Officer of Health of Croydon the advantages of working directly with family doctors outweigh this drawback: furthermore, doctors there are tending to confine acceptance of new patients to those living nearer, and thus solving the major problem of nurse attachment.

Mental welfare. Perhaps the most outstanding developments in the boroughs have taken place in the field of mental welfare. Thus in Bromley the number of referrals rose from 265 in 1965 to 421 in 1966, and total cases in care from 598 to 829, while in Waltham Forest the number of interviews with patients doubled over the same period.

There has been great activity in the provision and planning of provision of adult and junior training centres for the mentally subnormal, and of senior and junior hostels, workshops, social centres and hostels for the mentally ill. Some figures relating to these developments, extracted from the Ministry of Health's *Health and Welfare*, will be found later. This publication, however, makes no mention of 'special care units' for low-grade children, many also physically handicapped, who are capable of receiving basic care and habit training. These units, which afford great relief of family tensions and considerably benefit the children, were formerly to be found almost exclusively in the Middlesex area, but a number of other boroughs, including Bromley, Wandsworth and Westminster, are now providing them. Other innovations are the provision of a training centre for the doubly handicapped by Lewisham, which also provides occupational therapy for the mentally ill, and, by Wandsworth, of flatlets for the mentally ill in association with their hostel to prevent this becoming blocked, and as a final step towards independence.

A particular feature of the development of the mental health service is the closer relationship being established with the mental hospitals. In Redbridge, there is a combined mental-health social-work department, serving both the borough and the local psychiatric and general hospitals.

WELFARE SERVICES

The aged. Two of the most unsatisfactory features of the former administrative system of welfare for the elderly were the presence of large numbers of old people in the old Poor Law Institutions, and the maldistribution of small homes – a number of the new boroughs found themselves without any of the latter within their boundaries. Plans have been made to abolish all the old institutions by 1975, and to build large numbers of small homes (some details of these plans will be found below), but progress is slow owing to government restrictions. Nevertheless, some boroughs have succeeded in providing new homes. In a new Bromley home, residents have been permitted to bring in their own furniture, and this has proved so successful that the experiment is to be repeated in the next home built.

Short-term care and day care of old people in the homes is being increasingly undertaken in order to relieve relatives. In Bromley, the number of short term cases received in 1966 was double that of 1965, while day care attendances rose from 132 to 1,136. Greenwich also makes use of a teachers' training college during vacation for this purpose.

Short stay care of this kind is but one of the means adopted to attain the generally recognised ideal of keeping old people in their own homes as long as possible. Other means are meals on wheels, lunch clubs, day centres, as well as home helps and home nurses, and social visiting by volunteers and welfare officers. Camden, for example, has a staff of twenty employed exclusively for domiciliary visiting to the aged. Increasing use is everywhere being made of all these expedients. As a result, the average age of the aged in homes maintained by councils is steadily rising, but because the number of the old is also still increasing, and the demand for accommodation grows rather than lessens, nearly all boroughs have long waiting lists, and all regret that there cannot be speedier provision of new homes.

Sheltered housing in flatlets with wardens is another means of forestalling the need for residential accommodation in homes or hospitals. Little of this sort of provision has been made in the London area, but it is now steadily growing. Bromley, for example, now provides 301 units of this kind, and in addition has made grants amounting to £4,500 in respect of such accommodation for ninety-five old people. Here the fact that housing and welfare in the London boroughs are under the control of one authority has certainly helped.

The physically handicapped. While there has undoubtedly been a large increase in the visitation of the old and in the endeavour to ascertain those at risk (some boroughs keep lists of these), there are no figures to show the extent of the increase. In the case of the physically handicapped, however, such figures are available, and the increase in the number registered is most striking (see below, p. 137). This is certainly due to more effective ascertainment and the readier local availability of services.

In addition, there has been a marked increase in the provision of transport facilities, and growing numbers of work and recreational centres are being provided to give the handicapped an opportunity of leading fuller lives. An example of initiative in securing this end is afforded by Hillingdon which has started a gardening class for the handicapped. A growing number of boroughs are seeking to provide opportunities for paid employment.

The homeless. Perhaps the most striking transformation in welfare services has been in the provision for the homeless. Before 1965 this had been dealt with mainly as a mass problem of temporary accommodation by welfare departments.[1] Buildings, generally old Poor Law Institutions, were adapted to house up to sixty or more families. A searching comment on this type of accommodation for this purpose has been made by one of the boroughs. 'A large block of dwellings accommodating sixty families of all categories is not the most suitable means of providing temporary accommodation. Families who have been used to a good standard of housing are discontented with their surroundings, whilst those who may be more easily influenced by their neighbours tend to lower rather than raise their standards.' Incidentally, the use of large units means that they draw their residents from a wide area, complicating problems of travel to work for husbands and of school attendance for children, and removing wives from their normal contacts with neighbours and their local shops.

Accordingly, there is a general move to discontinue the use of the larger establishments. This is proceeding most rapidly in the outer boroughs where the homeless problem is less acute. Boroughs have already discontinued use of the establishments of the Kent County Council at West Malling, and Essex County Council at Hornchurch. In inner London, Southwark no longer uses Morning Lane, Hackney, where it has a claim on some of the seventy units of accommodation.

There is, in fact, a marked difference in the homeless problem between inner London (the former L.C.C. area) and outer, both in the size and the manner of dealing with it. At the end of the September quarter, 1967, there were 1,711 families (8,308 persons) in temporary accommodation in Greater London, of whom only

[1] It should be mentioned that shortly before the change over the London County Council, acting on the recommendation of a research study which they commissioned from the London School of Economics, transferred responsibility for the homeless from the welfare to the housing department.

378 (1,800) were in outer London, though this has the larger population, an indication of the much greater seriousness of the problem in inner London.

As regards methods, some of the pre-reform authorities in outer London preferred to deal with their homeless problem themselves as housing authorities rather than refer cases to the county welfare department. This readiness to regard homelessness as a housing problem persists. Thus in the September Quarter, 1967, total applications for temporary accommodation in inner London numbered 1,098 and in outer London 654, with 335 (31 per cent) and 129 (20 per cent) admissions respectively. But, in addition, in outer London 171 families were rehoused directly by housing departments without having made application for admission. The number so rehoused in inner London was seven.

Both the Greater London Council and the London Borough Councils, however, also allocate housing vacancies to families in temporary accommodation, the numbers so rehoused in the same quarter being as follows:

	Inner London	Outer London
Rehoused by G.L.C.	44	1
Rehoused by London boroughs	106	57
Rehoused before admission (see above)	7	171
	157	229

It will be seen that over the period considerably more families were rehoused by the authorities in outer than in inner London – a reflection of the easier housing situation there, but as is pointed out by Sutton, homelessness often reflects not so much lack of housing as the inadequacies of those who are already housed.

In this connection, the general use of smaller units of accommodation also facilitates the special provision both in inner and outer London for particular types of family such as the unmarried mother with her child, the family with only a single parent, and the so-called problem family. Many boroughs are now maintaining these specialised units. There has also been a much larger allocation of social workers dealing specifically with the homeless.[1] These are concerned not only with those in temporary accommodation, but are also engaged in preventive work among those not actually homeless, but at risk of becoming so through arrears of rent, etc., who may be referred through health visitors, child care officers and others. Harrow, thus, during 1966 had had twenty-two cases referred

[1] Westminster also has a social worker specifically for immigrants.

I

from the Arrears Sub-committee of the Housing Committee; six of these were out of debt and regularly paying their way, two had moved, and in only one case was no progress made.

While some boroughs report a reduction in the number of families provided with temporary accommodation, overall the number has increased. The increase over fifteen months is 12 per cent overall (11 per cent in inner London, 25 per cent in outer London).

	Number Accommodated June Quarter 1966		Number Accommodated September Quarter 1967	
	Families	Persons	Families	Persons
Inner London	1,207	5,845	1,333	6,505
Outer London	304	1,440	378	1,800
Total	1,511	7,285	1,711	8,305

These figures are from the quarterly returns of the Research and Intelligence Department of the G.L.C. Rather longer-range figures are available from the I.M.T.A. Welfare Statistics.

AVERAGE NUMBERS IN TEMPORARY ACCOMMODATION

	1963–4	Average cost per 1,000 population	1966–7	Average cost per 1,000 population
County of London	4,877	£91 9s.		
Inner London boroughs			5,672	£126 5s.
County of Middlesex	765	£19 7s.		
Middlesex boroughs[1]			877	£19 2s.

Whatever the discrepancies between these two sets of figures, both certainly indicate an increase in the number in temporary accommodation (and also an increase in cost in inner London), and this might be regarded as a failure on the part of the new authorities.

This would be an unjustified conclusion to draw, first because the housing problem is still acute, second because there was a considerable element of deterrence in the provision made by the previous authorities. Press attacks on Kent's West Malling establishment and on some of those in London will be remembered.

A fair estimate of the situation would be that a greater effort is now being made in solving the housing problem. Where these problems are due to inadequacies of individual families, more strenuous efforts are being made to educate them up to better standards.

CHILDREN'S DEPARTMENTS

Evidence of initiative and experimentation in the new children's

[1] See footnotes p. 132.

departments is hard to find. For this the reason is undoubtedy shortage of staff. The increase in the demand for qualified child care officers, together with the increase in the number of departments from nine to thirty-two, coupled with a national shortage of supply, has resulted in practically every borough being below establishment. This means that existing staff are wholly preoccupied with the attempt to keep up with the increasing volume of routine work, since the number in care per 1,000 population under eighteen has gone up from 12·2 (L.C.C. 1963–4) to 14·5 (inner London boroughs 1966–7) although remaining practically stationary in the former Middlesex area.[1] One hope, that the low proportion of children boarded out in inner London might rise, has not been realised, the percentage having dropped from twenty-seven to twenty-five, though it has risen from thirty-five to thirty-nine in the Middlesex boroughs.[1]

Perhaps as a result of this pressure of routine work, there is evidence of much greater co-operation in dealing with family problems between the children's and other social welfare departments than existed in some of the former authorities, where there was a tendency by the children's department to claim the status of a family welfare service which caused some resentment. Here the factor of size also enters in – interdepartmental communication is generally easier in smaller authorities, while interdepartmental rivalry tends to be endemic in larger ones.

THE STATISTICAL PICTURE

It is clear from the foregoing pages that the new London boroughs are showing a great deal of energy, initiative and enterprise in tackling their new tasks, and that this is a general attitude, not confined to those in either inner or outer London, or to the larger, richer or more influential among them.

It may well be urged, however, that the picture given is a subjective one, that action taken has often resulted from the promptings of Ministry circulars, that this sort of development is taking place all over the country, and that the former authorities, had they continued to exist, might have done as much.

What is needed, it will be said, to justify a contention that the reforms have improved the standard of the services, is some hard figures enabling comparisons to be made between pre- and post-reform performance in London, and between present-day performance by the London boroughs and by the county boroughs, their nearest counterparts in the rest of the country.

[1] I.M.T.A. Children's Statistics, see below, p. 140.

	London C.C. 31.3.64	Inner London Boroughs[1] 31.3.65	Middlesex C.C. 31.3.64	Middlesex Boroughs[2] 31.3.65
HEALTH				
No. of Health Centres	2	4	0	0
Field staff per 100,000 *population*				
Health visitors	15	15	11	12
Home nurses	16	18	13	14
Home helps	89	91	45	42
Social workers	10	16	9	7
Mentally subnormal				
Places per 100,000 pop.				
—in adult training centres	23	21	28	27
—in junior training centres	10	11	35	29
No. of hostels	1	4	2	2
Mentally ill				
No. of workshops	2	7	1	1
No. of centres	3	11	3	3
No. of hostels	1	2	3	4
WELFARE				
The elderly				
Places in homes per 1,000 pop. (65 and over)	22	22	16	15
Average no. of places per home	150	136	61	60
No. of persons in special housing per 1,000 pop. (65 and over)	8·6	2·6	2·7	3·1
No. of centres	0	26	0	10
The physically handicapped				
No. of centres	13	40	114	60
No. of homes	4	3	2	2
The homeless				
No. of families provided for	1100	1544	142	141
No. of families per establishment	41	34	13	11

[1] Inner London Boroughs: the twelve boroughs covering the former L.C.C. area, viz. Camden, Greenwich, Hackney, Hammersmith, Islington, Kensington & Chelsea, Lambeth, Lewisham, Southwark, Tower Hamlets, Wandsworth and Westminster.

[2] Middlesex Boroughs: the nine London boroughs roughly corresponding to the area of the former county of Middlesex, viz. Barnet, Brent, Ealing, Enfield, Haringey, Harrow, Hillingdon, Hounslow, and Richmond upon Thames. The correspondence is not exact because

(a) *Barnet L.B.* includes Barnet U.D. (population 28,000) and East Barnet U.D. (41,000) which were formerly in Hertfordshire;

(b) *Richmond upon Thames L.B.* includes Richmond M.B. (41,000) and Barnes M.B. (40,000) which were formerly in Surrey;

(c) Potters Bar U.D. (23,000), Staines U.D. (43,000) and Sunbury-on-Thames

10 County Boroughs³ 31.3.65	London C.C. 31.3.74	Inner London Boroughs¹ 31.3.71	Middlesex C.C. 31.3.74	Middlesex Boroughs² 31.3.71	10 County Boroughs³ 31.3.71
4	2	13	0	18	24
13	24	19	16	17	19
17	17	20	17	17	19
73	118	109	70	56	95
9	17	27	12	11	13
51	41	45	68	52	88
41	9	18	34	48	59
10	3	11	16	13	24
2	9	14	9	4	2
6	18	12	3	15	8
2	2	9	19	11	9
19	24	28	16	22	24
54	85	76	56	47	47
7·8	—	6·3	—	10·3	16·2
14	0	68	—	30	39
36	23	60	131	79	37
6	4	6	2	5	9
76	—	1481	142	180	141
2·5	—	15	13	5	2·8

U.D. (33,000), all formerly in Middlesex, were not included in Greater London.

The net effect is that, on the basis of the 1961 Census figures quoted, the nine L.B. include 150,000 people who were not in Middlesex and exclude 99,000 people who were. (1961 Census population for the whole of Middlesex was 2,231,000.) Although an exact comparison is thus not possible between pre-1965 Middlesex and post-1965 London boroughs, it is considered that the figures in the table are unlikely to be seriously misleading.

³ Ten County Boroughs: the ten English County Boroughs with populations between 200,000 and 350,000, i.e. corresponding to the population range within which most of the London boroughs fall, viz. Bradford, Coventry, Hull, Leicester, Newcastle upon Tyne, Nottingham, Plymouth, Portsmouth, Southampton and Stoke-on-Trent.

As has already been stated, some statistics are available from the Ministry of Health and from the Institute of Municipal Treasurers and Accountants and the Society of County Treasurers.

The Ministry of Health on three occasions asked local authorities to give details of their provision of certain health and welfare services in a given year, and their planned provisions for future years.[1] In the table on pp. 132–3 comparisons are made between the actual provision of the London and Middlesex County Councils in 1964 and the actual provision of the inner London boroughs and the Middlesex boroughs[2] in 1965; and between the planned provision of the two counties for 1974 and that of the boroughs for 1971.

The I.M.T.A. produce statistics annually, from which are derived the figures given in the table comparing county performance in 1963–4 and London borough performance in 1966–7.

Figures are also given of the performance of ten English county boroughs at corresponding dates.

These figures are all derived from returns made by the authorities, and are probably as reliable as most statistics compiled in this way, but by no means infallible. Mention will be made below of instances where obvious errors have crept in or where comparisons are clearly invalid.

Health centres. Any comparison between the plans for the provision of health centres made by the counties of London and Middlesex and those made by the boroughs which replaced them would clearly be unfair to the former, since the revived interest in health centres took place after the London Government reforms. In fact, Middlesex had none and planned none, and London had two but planned no increase.

The danger of accepting published statistics wholly at their face value is illustrated by the figures relating to health centres. In *Health and Welfare* there were said to be four in one outer borough in 1965 but enquiry showed that none of these was a health centre as now understood. On the other hand, another outer borough was stated to have none, but already had two in action.

Twenty of the thirty-two London boroughs (62·5 per cent) plan to have forty-three health centres between them by 1971. Of ten county boroughs of comparable size, five (50 per cent) have planned for twenty-four centres. Of the eighty-one county boroughs in England and Wales, thirty (37 per cent) have plans for seventy-two.

[1] In the first survey: provision in 1962, plans for 1972; in the second: provision in 1963 and 1964, plans for 1969 and 1974; in the third: provision in 1965, plans for 1971 and 1976.

[2] See footnote p. 132 for definition of term 'Middlesex boroughs'.

Field staff. The most noticeable feature of the figures relating to field staff in the personal health services is the disparity between the standards of London and Middlesex C.C.s in 1964. The London borough figures of 1965 show little change, but while the inner London standards were generally well above those in the ten county boroughs, those in the Middlesex boroughs were generally well below. Nor does the planned provision look like remedying this disparity. Indeed the planned provision of home helps is only about half that of inner London, about two-thirds that of the ten county boroughs, and substantially less than that planned by the Middlesex County Council.

The 1974 plans of the L.C.C. and the 1971 plans of the inner London boroughs do not differ greatly, save that fewer health visitors are proposed by the boroughs, and more social workers.

The mentally handicapped. With regard to the mentally subnormal, in actual provision London has lagged behind Middlesex, and both behind the county boroughs. All authorities are planning an increase in the number of training centre places and the number of hostels, but it is noticeable that the percentage increase proposed by the London boroughs is higher at about 100 per cent than that of the county boroughs at 75 per cent, so that the gap is now narrowing. In the case of the inner London boroughs, the additions proposed are higher than those of the L.C.C. In general, the London boroughs are getting closer to the county borough standards, but there is still some way to go, especially in the provision of junior training centres in inner London.

In the provision of workshops, centres and hostels for the mentally ill, the inner London boroughs had already in 1965 shown a marked advance on the London County Council provision, and their planned provision for 1971 much exceeded that of the L.C.C. in 1974 in respect of workshops and hostels, though considerably lower in respect of centres. The figures of the Middlesex boroughs are less impressive, but still considerably exceed those of the county boroughs.

It should also be emphasised that a considerable proportion of social workers in the local health services are mental health workers, and it has already been mentioned that the inner London boroughs have largely increased the number of their social workers, and plan a further substantial increase. The Middlesex boroughs also plan an increase, but not so great, and not as great as that of the county boroughs.

Welfare of the elderly. Accepted requirements of homes for old people are first that there should be enough of them, and second, that they should not be too large, the old type of institution having been completely outmoded.

The County of London in 1964 provided twenty-two places per 1,000 persons of sixty-five or over, and planned twenty-four by 1974; Middlesex provided sixteen per 1,000 and planned sixteen. The inner London boroughs raised the target figure for 1971 to twenty-eight, and the Middlesex boroughs to twenty-two. The county borough target for 1971 was twenty-four (from nineteen in 1965), a figure between that of the two sets of London boroughs. But it is noticeable that the Middlesex boroughs were planning an increase of nearly 50 per cent, while that of the inner London boroughs and the county boroughs was about 25 per cent. In other words, the former were aiming to make up the leeway left them by the Middlesex C.C.

As regards size, the L.C.C. establishments were on the average nearly three times as large as those in the county boroughs, and more than twice as large as those in Middlesex. The county boroughs propose to reduce the size of their establishments by 13 per cent by 1971, the Middlesex boroughs by 22 per cent (which will bring them level with the county boroughs). The inner London boroughs propose a reduction of 56 per cent which will still leave them with considerably larger homes than those in Middlesex and the county boroughs, but which is indicative of the energy with which the matter is being tackled.

The figures in the table relating to special housing and to old people's centres are liable to give an entirely misleading impression. With regard to special housing, in London in 1964 all such housing was provided by the London County Council. The G.L.C. is still a housing authority and still provides such housing, but the 1965 inner London borough figures refer to provision made by the boroughs only. The G.L.C. and L.C.C. special housing for the old is not, however, generally warden-supervised, which is normally the case in the London and county boroughs. It will be seen that London has lagged behind the county boroughs in this provision, but that once again the leeway is being made up.

With regard to old people's centres, the two counties had an agreement with the second-tier authorities that in the division of responsibilities for the aged between them, this provision should be made by the metropolitan and municipal boroughs. A particularly noticeable development in this field is planned by the inner London boroughs.

The physically handicapped. There are three groups included in this category: the blind and partially sighted, the deaf and hard of hearing, and the otherwise physically handicapped, i.e. in the main,

the crippled. All three categories are liable to registration. Blind
registers have been in operation a long time, and are pretty complete. The only persons registered in the other two categories are
those actually assisted by the local authorities. The size of its
register is thus a fair indication of the activity of a local authority in
this sphere.

The following table (from I.M.T.A. Welfare Statistics, 1963–4 and
1966–7) shows the numbers of registered in the three groups in 1964
and 1967:

NUMBER AND TYPE OF DISABLED PERSONS ON REGISTER

	31.3.64			21.3.67		
	London C.C.	Middlesex C.C.	10 Large C.B.s	Inner L.B.s	Middlesex L.B.s	10 Large C.B.s
Blind and p.s.	9,719	5,016	7,442	9,904	5,631	8,017
Phys. hand.	8,971	4,959	8,322	15,773	7,775	11,382
Deaf, etc.	404	2,463	2,686	833	1,125	3,247

The outstanding feature here is the remarkable increase of 75 per
cent in the number of physically handicapped registered in inner
London.[1] There was also an increase in Middlesex (36 per cent) and
the county boroughs, but not nearly so marked.

As could be expected, the increase in registrations of the blind
was everywhere small. With regard to the deaf and dumb, the
anomaly here is the decrease in registrations in Middlesex. This
appears to be due to the fact that Middlesex County Council made a
practice of including cases registered with voluntary organisations
as well as those registered direct with the council.

A similar explanation accounts for the anomaly regarding the
provision of centres for the physically handicapped shown in the
table on page 133. The figures relate to provision for all types of
handicapped, and here again Middlesex C.C. appear to have included centres provided by voluntary organisations. The figures
again show a marked increase in both actual and planned provision
in inner London, and much more generous provision in London than
in the ten county boroughs.

The provision of homes for the disabled of all types is mainly
in the hands of voluntary organisations; the figures here, therefore,
are of little significance.

The homeless. Homelessness is not a major problem outside inner
London. Here the chief feature of the figures is the reduction already

[1] In Southwark the number practically trebled between March 1965 and June
1968, from 1,352 to nearly 3,900.

effected in the size of establishments for the homeless and the further reductions planned. The number of homeless has actually increased, which may be accounted for in some measure by the fact already mentioned that the former mass provision contained an element of deterrence.

Finance. The I.M.T.A. statistics enable some interesting comparisons to be made between the expenditure on the health and welfare services before and after the reforms:

AVERAGE NET EXPENDITURE PER 1,000 POPULATION (£s)

I. HEALTH SERVICES

	1963–4		1966–7	Increase (%)
L.C.C.	2,533	Inner L.B.s	2,823	11·5
Middlesex C.C.	1,817	Middlesex L.B.s	1,965	7·5
		(All L.B.s	2,294)	
All C.B.s	1,836	All C.B.s	2,408	32·0
10 Large C.B.s	1,930	10 Large C.B.s	2,601	35·0

II. WELFARE SERVICES

L.C.C.	1,555	Inner L.B.s	1,840	18·0
Middlesex C.C.	740	Middlesex L.B.s	1,192	61·0
		(All L.B.s	1,429)	
All C.B.s	866	All C.B.s	1,181	36·0
10 Large C.B.s	817	10 Large C.B.s	1,185	45·0

It will be seen that the London County Council spent very considerably more per 1,000 population than the county boroughs on both health and welfare services, and the Middlesex County Council rather less.

By 1967 the county boroughs were spending about a third more on both services, the large ones rather more. In London, the new boroughs had also increased expenditure on both services, but in respect of the welfare services in inner London only by 18 per cent, as compared with the county boroughs' 36 per cent, while in the Middlesex boroughs there was an increase of 60 per cent, which brought them into line with the county boroughs. The inner London boroughs' expenditure was still considerably higher than the county boroughs', but now by only 55 per cent instead of 78 per cent.

A somewhat similar picture emerges in respect of the health services, except that the Middlesex boroughs have increased their expenditure only slightly, with the result that the expenditure of the London boroughs as a whole is rather below that of the county boroughs.

Children's Services. In respect of children virtually the only statistical source available is the I.M.T.A. In their statistics, the outstanding feature is the very much higher proportion of children taken into care in Central London than elsewhere:

	Total children in care	Average no. in care per 1,000 children under 18	
		1963–4	1966–7
County of London	9,493	12·2	—
Inner L.B.s	9,922	—	14·5
County of Middlesex	2,866	5·3	—
Middlesex L.B.s	2,867	—	5·2
10 Large C.B.s	4,802	6·6	—
10 Large C.B.s	5,447	—	7·6

The marked contrast between the proportion of deprived children in the inner London boroughs and in the Middlesex boroughs is due to the difference in the social structure. Middlesex has a settled and more middle-class population with large residential areas, inner London a more transient and cosmopolitan population and large working-class areas. Greater London as a whole has 8·0 children in care per 1,000 under eighteen, comparable with the ten county boroughs (7·6).

The total cost of the children's service in inner London is therefore very much higher than elsewhere, but the average cost per child is not now much more than in the Middlesex area, though in both cases it has increased considerably, is well above that in the ten large county boroughs, and is increasing rapidly:

AVERAGE COST PER CHILD IN CARE (£)

	1963–4	1966–7	Increase (%)
L.C.C.	510	—	—
Inner L.B.s	—	683	34
Middlesex C.C.	405	—	—
Middlesex L.B.s	—	606	50
10 Large C.B.s	379	478	26

One reason for the higher cost per child in Greater London is the lower percentage of children boarded out. The average cost per child week of boarding out to all authorities in England and Wales in 1966–7 was 62s. 1d.; in inner London, 72s. 8d., in the county boroughs 61s. 11d. The cost per child week in local authority homes, nurseries and hostels was 260s. 7d.; in London boroughs, 317s. 4d., county boroughs, 237s. 5d. Not only is boarding out cheaper; more important, it is generally regarded as a happier method of treatment wherever practicable.

Clearly boarding out from inner London presents far greater difficulties than in other parts of the country and the proportion so dealt with has always been low. It was hoped that with the advent of smaller authorities this proportion might be increased, but this has not happened:

PERCENTAGE OF CHILDREN BOARDED OUT

	1963–4	1966–7
L.C.C.	27	—
Inner L.B.s	—	25
Middlesex C.C.	35	—
Middlesex L.B.s	—	39
C.B.s	51	49
All L.B.s	—	31

The proportion boarded out in Middlesex has increased but is still well below that of the county boroughs. There are wide variations in the London boroughs. Thus the percentage for Harrow was 66, Redbridge 65, Croydon 57 and Newham, although comprising a poor area near the centre, 50. On the other hand the percentage in Kensington & Chelsea was 18 and in Westminster 16. But these last two made extensive use of voluntary homes where the average cost to local authorities per child week is much lower than in their own homes (109s. 6d. as against 237s. 5d. in Greater London).

Taking the inner London boroughs and Middlesex boroughs separately and comparing the cost of their homes with those of the London and Middlesex C.C.s and C.B.s, the figures are as follows:

	Children's Homes			Residential Nurseries		
	Cost*	Increase (%)	Average occupation rate	Cost*	Increase (%)	Average occupation rate
L.C.C. 1963–4	243	—	94	305	—	97
Inner L.B. 1966–7	307	26	85	408	34	91
Middlesex C.C. 1963–4	171	—	80	299	—	88
Middlesex L.B.s 1966–7	263	54	80	341	14	92
C.B.s 1963–4	188	—	N.A.	289	—	N.A.
C.B.s 1966–7	215	14	N.A.	361	24	N.A.

* Shillings per child week.

It will be seen that a contributory factor in the increased cost in the inner London boroughs in both homes and residential nurseries has been the lower average occupation. Costs in the Middlesex homes have risen sharply with the same average occupation, but were low in 1963–4 under Middlesex C.C. In residential nurseries with a high occupation rate, the rise in costs in Middlesex has been small and is now below that in the county boroughs.

Finally, a large increase has been shown in London under the I.M.T.A. heading 'general expenditure', amounting to around one-quarter of the total expenditure of all authorities, and presumably covering administration.

GENERAL EXPENSES PER 1,000 POPULATION

	£	Increase (%)
L.C.C. 1963–4	253	—
Inner L.B.s 1966–7	595	135
Middlesex C.C. 1963–4	88	—
Middlesex L.B.s 1966–7	213	148
All L.B.s 1966–7	356	—
All C.B.s 1963–4	118	—
All C.B.s 1966–7	204	73

The fact that the costs are absolutely so much higher in inner London than elsewhere is due in part at any rate to the greater numbers in care, but it appears that the cost of administration in London following the reforms has increased twice as much as in the county boroughs.

The general impression left by this limited statistical survey is that the London reforms have been less successful in the field of children's work than in health and welfare. Costs are certainly higher. Figures give little indication of the quality of service, but those regarding boarding out suggest that there has been no general improvement here. If so, the cause is likely to be the great difficulty in recruitment of staff by the London boroughs.[1]

ENTERTAINMENT AND THE ARTS

A service of a rather different kind, formerly the responsibility of the pre-reform authorities and now carried out by the new London boroughs and the G.L.C., is the provision of entertainment and support of the arts.

It was not until 1948, under the Local Government Act of that year, that local authorities were free to provide entertainment and support the arts in their areas, up to a net cost not exceeding the equivalent of a 6d. rate.

Before the London Government reforms a study was made of the extent to which local authorities were availing themselves of this power in the Greater London area.[2] It has therefore been possible

[1] For an illustration of this point, see Royal Commission on Local Government in England, Research Study 2, *The Lessons of the London Government Reforms*, pp. 22–3.

[2] *Municipal Entertainment and the Arts in Greater London*, S. K. Ruck (London, George Allen & Unwin).

to ascertain what effect the reforms have had in this particular field, as a contrast to the major statutory services considered earlier in this chapter.

In 1960–1 the authorities then in power in the present Greater London area spent £1,266,000 on Entertainment and the Arts. Of this sum the Metropolitan boroughs and the City contributed £140,000, the outer authorities (those outside the County of London) £214,000 and the London County Council itself £912,000.

In 1966–7 the inner London boroughs and the City spent £365,000, the outer Boroughs £498,000, and the G.L.C. £1,713,000, a total of £2,576,000. This total is in fact an underestimate, since three authorities, one in inner and two in outer London, did not reply to enquiries, whereas all replied re 1960–1. None of the authorities comprised in these boroughs at the earlier date in fact made any great expenditure in this field, and this fact, coupled with the lack of interest shown in the enquiry, suggests they were not substantial spenders in 1966–7.

LOCAL AUTHORITIES IN GREATER LONDON
Expenditure on and Income from Entertainment and the Arts,
1960–1 *and* 1966–7

A. INNER LONDON

London Borough	Former Authorities	Expenditure £			Income £		
		1960–1	Total 1960–1	1966–7	1960–1	Total 1960–1	1966–7
Camden	Hampstead	3,408 ⎫			— ⎫		
	St Pancras	14,730 ⎬	19,393	64,346	1,514 ⎬	1,514	14,557
	Holborn	1,255 ⎭			— ⎭		
Greenwich	Greenwich	177 ⎫			— ⎫		
	Woolwich	6,326 ⎭	6,503	38,168	350 ⎭	350	1,108
Hackney	Hackney	9,363 ⎫			2,889 ⎫		
	Stoke Newington	1,319 ⎬	11,732	10,560	— ⎬	2,889	1,328
	Shoreditch	1,050 ⎭			— ⎭		
Hammersmith	Hammersmith	8,650 ⎫			1,356 ⎫		
	Fulham	10,039 ⎭	18,644	59,240	1,724 ⎭	3,080	3,755
Islington	Islington	4,991 ⎫			390 ⎫		
	Finsbury	3,993 ⎭	8,984	10,065	1,915 ⎭	2,305	340
Kensington & Chelsea	Kensington	4,446 ⎫			— ⎫		
	Chelsea	200 ⎭	4,646	1,678	— ⎭	—	—
Lewisham	Lewisham	3,023 ⎫			251 ⎫		
	Deptford	125 ⎭	3,148	29,544	— ⎭	251	10,388
Southwark	Southwark	7,014 ⎫			289 ⎫		
	Bermondsey	6,810 ⎬	26,979	27,763	2,134 ⎬	2,662	4,233
	Camberwell	13,155 ⎭			239 ⎭		
Tower Hamlets	Stepney	2,174 ⎫			— ⎫		
	Bethnal Green	1,600 ⎬	7,935	NR	679 ⎬	4,122	NR
	Poplar	4,161 ⎭			3,443 ⎭		
Westminster	Westminster	97 ⎫			— ⎫		
	St Marylebone	— ⎬	306	20,762	— ⎬	—	825
	Paddington	209 ⎭			— ⎭		
Wandsworth	Wandsworth	551			—		
Lambeth	Lambeth	2,013 ⎫			50 ⎫		
	Battersea	8,704 ⎭	11,286	34,704	3,124 ⎭	3,174	2,380
City of London			20,132	68,073		—	—

B. OUTER LONDON

Barking	Barking	1,866 ⎫			— ⎫		
	Dagenham	9,051 ⎭	10,917	21,844	7,311 ⎭	7,311	5,301

London Borough	Former Authorities	Expenditure £ 1960–1	Total 1960–1	1966–7	Income £ 1960–1	Total 1960–1	1966–7
Barnet	Barnet	331			—		
	East Barnet	—			—		
	Friern Barnet	1,458	6,137	7,159	1,091	1,091	27
	Finchley	199			—		
	Hendon	4.148			—		
Bexley	Erith	876			—		
	Bexley	1,281	2,771	NR	—	313	NR
	Crayford	614			313		
Brent	Wembley	10,527	38,332	110,710	14,787	24,447	54,114
	Willesden	27,805			9,660		
Bromley	Penge	—			—		
	Beckenham	124			—		
	Bromley	1,574	2,587	11,125	—	—	—
	Orpington	—			—		
	Chislehurst & Sidcup	889			—		
Croydon	Croydon	28,763	28,781	193.208	—	—	118,350
	Coulsdon & Purley	18			—		
Ealing	Ealing	8,433			3,721		
	Acton	4,512	21,126	30,520	366	8,219	5,967
	Southall	8,181			3,132		
Enfield	Enfield	10,030			2,537		
	Edmonton	11,460	22,397	31,134	1,935	4,544	10,460
	Southgate	907			72		
Haringey	Wood Green	1,147			50		
	Tottenham	13,442	15,810	26,000	3,792	3,842	8,080
	Hornsey	1,221			—		
Harrow	Harrow		652	1,700		—	—
Havering	Romford	1,611	9,398	18,950	—	90	—
	Hornchurch	7,787			90		
Hillingdon	Ruislip-Northwood	354			—		
	Uxbridge	742			—		
	Hayes & Harlington	5,037	6,151	NR	2,116	2,116	NR
	Yiewsley & W. Drayton	18			—		
Hounslow	Heston & Isleworth	134			—		
	Feltham	494	1,368	2,500	—	62	—
	Brentford & Chiswick	740			62		
Kingston upon Thames	Kingston	3,495			—		
	Surbiton	—	3,495	775	—	—	351
	Malden & Coombe	—			—		
Merton	Merton & Morden	1,258			—		
	Mitcham	—	1,258	3,233	—	—	29
	Wimbledon	—			—		
Newham	East Ham	233	4,505	2,500	—	—	—
	West Ham	4,272			—		
Redbridge	Ilford	4,978	4,978	5,665	1,995	1,995	48
	Wanstead & Woodford	—			—		
Richmond upon Thames	Richmond	40			—		
	Twickenham	550	646	2,546	—	—	—
	Barnes	56			—		
Sutton	Sutton & Cheam	1,942			782		
	Carshalton	747	2,689	3,807	67	859	807
	Beddington & Wallington	—			—		
Waltham Forest	Walthamstow	21,708			8,941		
	Leyton	9,161	31,283	24,913	5,618	14,735	5,896
	Chingford	414			176		

C. SUMMARY

	Expenditure £ 1960–1	1966–7	Income £ 1960–1	1966–7
Inner London	139,660	364,903	20,347	38,914
Outer London	214,392	498,289	71,674	204,120
L.C.C.	911,962	—	362,855	—
G.L.C.	—	1,713,000	—	359,000
TOTAL	1,266,014	2,576,192	454,876	602,030

It appears then that London local authorities were spending twice as much on this provision in 1966–7 as their predecessors. Part of the increase may have taken place before 1965, part may be due to inflation, but it is clear that the new authorities as a whole are doing more in this field than their predecessors.

Of the twenty-nine boroughs which made returns, two had a *gross* expenditure of over £100,000 in 1966–7, two between £50,000 and £100,000, eleven £20,000–£50,000, four £10,000–£20,000, and ten under £10,000. Only two boroughs had a net expenditure exceeding the product of a penny rate. It will thus be seen that there were wide differences in performance in this field.

Generally speaking, when there was activity in any one or more of the constituent authorities in 1960–1, this activity had nearly always increased and sometimes increased greatly in 1966–7, thus spreading the effects over a wider area. Where there was little activity at the earlier date, there was generally little later. On the other hand, one or two boroughs actually spent more (e.g. the Bromley authorities £2,000 in 1960–1, Bromley £11,000 in 1966–7; Westminster £21,000 in 1966–7, but Westminster, Paddington and Marylebone together only £300 in 1960–1).

The emphasis on cultural and popular entertainment varies considerably. Of the four biggest spenders all provide both types, but more cultural productions are to be found in Camden and Croydon, and more popular entertainment in Brent and Hammersmith. Croydon and Brent are exceptional in setting a substantial income against their expenditure, Croydon recovering more than half, Brent nearly half. One or two other authorities recover about a third, but most recover very little.

It might be expected that the boroughs most distant from the middle of London would be readier to spend more on the entertainment of their residents than those to which the West End is readily accessible. Broadly speaking, the reverse is the case; it is generally the boroughs on the periphery which spend least. And, once again speaking in general terms, their expenditure is largely in the form of grants to amateur societies and more particularly to Arts Councils which most boroughs support.

With regard to the future, the boroughs and the G.L.C. between them estimated an expenditure of £2,899,000 in 1967–8 as against £2,576,000 actually spent in 1966–7, or about £320,000 more. Thus the trend is towards a continual increase, but once again it was those who were spending most who proposed to spend more: those making little provision generally showed no disposition to increase it.

The attempt has been made in this chapter to give a *general* picture of how some of the more important of the London boroughs' functions are operating in the new administrative set-up. Pioneering efforts by individual boroughs have been mentioned, but while it is obvious that some boroughs are less effective than others in some fields, no attempt has been made to single these out.

It may be said broadly that a fairly uniform level of performance has been achieved in the older services, in part because they are concerned with functions of which local government has had long experience, in part also perhaps because of the control exercised by central government.

It is in the newer services like the Children's Service and Entertainment and the Arts, that marked variations of standard are to be found. Experienced and capable officials in these fields are harder to come by than in the old local government functions, and where they exist, are generally the standard setters.

K

Chapter VII

AUTHORITIES FOR SPECIAL PURPOSES

So far we have considered London's government almost entirely in terms of the local authorities with powers and duties in the metropolis. There are, however, two other principal means by which London is governed; the first is through agencies of the central government, the second through bodies specially set up to administer particular aspects of government.

The first will not be dealt with here. This is because the *system* of government is no different from elsewhere, although its *application* may differ in certain cases. The Post Office, the Regional Hospital Boards and the Electricity Boards, for example, all have their London organisations which do not differ in principle from those to be found elsewhere in the country. London has, however, because of its size and other peculiarities, compelled practical modifications in certain cases. Thus there was the familiar and distinctive London Postal Area with its district numbers, S.W.1, N.17, and so on; and because of the great concentration of Teaching Hospitals in Central London, Regional Hospital Board areas cover segments of London rather than being based on one central city containing a single teaching hospital as is usual in the provinces.[1]

The second group of authorities calls for rather more comment, because they each represent an attempt to deal with one particular London problem. For this reason we have borrowed the Webbs' term[2] to designate this class of *ad hoc* bodies, of which the three main representatives are the Metropolitan Police, the Metropolitan Water Board and London Transport.

THE METROPOLITAN POLICE (M.P.)

Reference was briefly made earlier[3] to the establishment of the Metropolitan Police by Peel's Act of 1829, and it was made clear that

[1] For a brief account of the position, see *Encyclopaedia Britannica*, 1967 edition, Article 'London, Government and Services'.

[2] Sidney and Beatrice Webb, *Statutory Authorities for Special Purposes* (London, Longmans, Green, 1922; reprinted, London, Frank Cass, 1963).

[3] Above, p. 16.

this was in response to the particular conditions prevailing in the metropolis. The Metropolitan Police has remained a unique force,[1] but it must not be assumed that this was a necessary and inevitable result. In 1839 a Royal Commission on policing in the counties reported in favour of a single national police force under the control of the Commissioners of the Metropolitan Police, but this proposal made no progress in the face of political opposition. Again, in 1839 police forces on the metropolitan model were established in Birmingham, Manchester and Bolton but soon reverted to the normal borough pattern of control by the Watch Committee.[2] If either of these approaches had met with more success the history of the Metropolitan Police might have turned out very differently.

The essential distinguishing feature of the force is still that ultimate responsibility for it rests with the Home Secretary and not with a police committee of the local authority.[3] This may have been inevitable in the circumstances of 1829, when there was no precedent for the organisation of an effective police force over such a large area. With the introduction of county and borough forces during the nineteenth century there was some demand (e.g. from the L.C.C.) that the Metropolitan Police too should be subject to some measure of local authority control. Nothing came of these demands, partly because there was no local authority whose area was anything like as large as the Metropolitan Police District. Furthermore, the unique nature of the Metropolitan Police was justified by its unique responsibilities; these included the protection of the Sovereign and of Parliament, duties of a national kind which were held to justify central government control of the force. The argument was advanced as recently as 1962 when there were already plans to create a Greater London Council with an area practically coextensive with the Metropolitan Police District. In that year, the Royal Commission on the Police said:

'We accept that there are overriding advantages in a unitary system of control over the police in the Metropolis and also that, in view of the exceptional police responsibilities in London, control should be in the hands of the Government.'[4]

---

[1] It must be remembered that the Metropolitan Police has no jurisdiction in the City of London, which retains its separate police force.

[2] On this, see T. A. Critchley, *A History of Police in England and Wales*, 900–1966 (London, Constable, 1967), pp. 74–87; also, Royal Commission on the Police, *Final Report* (Cmnd. 1728, 1962), para. 46.

[3] On police arrangements generally, see Critchley, op. cit.: also, J. M. Hart, *The British Police* (London, Allen & Unwin, 1951).

[4] Cmnd. 1728, para. 223.

They went on to argue that recent proposals for the reorganisation of local government in Greater London should not alter this position.

Nor has there been any pressure from the Greater London Council to take over the Metropolitan Police. Government, Parliament and the local authorities seem reasonably content with the present arrangements in spite of the fact that they leave the country's largest local authority with no say in the administration of the country's largest police force. That there must, however, be close co-operation between the G.L.C. and the Metropolitan Police is obvious in view of their complementary roles in the control of London's traffic. This is recognised in the proposal to establish a Joint Traffic Executive with representatives of the two authorities.[1]

Although ultimate responsibility for the force rests with the Home Secretary, he is not responsible for day-to-day administration and operational control. This is the duty of the Commissioner of the Metropolitan Police who is appointed by the Crown. Under the 1829 Act the creation and administration of the force were entrusted to two justices of the peace, specially appointed for that purpose by the Sovereign and known as Commissioners of Police of the Metropolis. This curious arrangement lasted until 1856 when the present arrangement of a single Commissioner was instituted. Under the Commissioner there is a Deputy Commissioner and four Assistant Commissioners, all of whom are also appointed by the Crown on the recommendation of the Home Secretary.

The formal relationship between the Home Secretary and the Commissioner is that the former controls the general policy of the force,[2] and the latter its operation. In practice, the limits of the Commissioner's responsibility are not precisely defined. Perhaps the most that can be said is that:

'It is difficult to delineate in a few words the respective spheres of the Home Secretary and Commissioner which in any event vary from time to time according to the personalities concerned.'[3]

By and large the Commissioner exercises the same powers as a chief constable elsewhere, e.g. he appoints the members of the force, but (i) he has certain additional powers which elsewhere are the responsibility of the police authority (e.g. licensing of taxis); (ii) he can be given instructions by the Home Secretary, although such instructions are normally confined to matters of general policy.

[1] *Transport in London* (Cmnd. 3686, H.M.S.O., 1968), para. 64.
[2] For example, orders and regulations of the Commissioner are subject to the Home Secretary's approval.
[3] Hart, op. cit., p. 115.

The Commissioner is not, however, solely responsible for the administration of the Metropolitan Police. The Receiver of the Metropolitan Police District has a status independent of the Commissioner and, like him, is appointed by the Crown on the recommendation of the Home Secretary. Until 1968 he was entirely concerned with the administration of the Metropolitan Police Fund and of all police property.[1] He was in effect the financial controller of the force, putting forward to the Home Secretary for approval proposals for new expenditure and laying before Parliament annually an account of income and expenditure, which, like the accounts of Government departments, is audited by the Comptroller and Auditor-General for the Public Accounts Committee.

Thus statutorily speaking the Commissioner and the Receiver are each responsible in their separate spheres to the Home Secretary. One consequence is that the latter 'settles any difference of opinion between the Commissioner and the Receiver on a financial matter'.[2] This arrangement has no parallel in any other police force in the country, and was no doubt intended as a safeguard under the original Act to ensure strict financial accountability. The Receiver is, therefore, neither a civil servant nor a member of the Commissioner's staff but a statutory officer. In practice, the trend increasingly in recent years has been to appoint as Receivers senior administrative civil servants from the Home Office.[3]

Little attention has been paid to this unusual feature of the Metropolitan Police, perhaps because it is only one of the ways in which the force differs from other police forces. One part of the financial arrangements has aroused criticism from the local authorities. Until recently, the Receiver was under no obligation to consult or otherwise inform local authorities of his statements of expenditure before they were laid before Parliament. This was important to the local authorities because the Receiver's estimates were the basis of the rate precept for police purposes which is fixed by the Home Secretary. Nor is it a negligible sum since local authorities contribute nearly half the cost of the force. The Metropolitan Boroughs' Standing Joint Committee raised the matter with the Royal Commission on the Police, who recommended[4] that there should be 'confidential consultation' between the Receiver and the local auth-

---

[1] For more recent developments, see below, p. 151.

[2] Hart, op. cit., p. 119.

[3] For example, Mr W. H. Cornish, who was Receiver from 1961 to 1967, had previously been Under Secretary in charge of the Police Division in the Home Office.

[4] Cmnd. 1728, para. 227.

orities before the estimates were presented to Parliament, and this is now done.

The Metropolitan Police Force consists at present of approximately 20,600 men and women out of an authorised establishment of 26,550.[1] There are in addition over 7,300 full-time 'civil staff', including clerks, typists and traffic wardens as well as professional and technical staff. In some ways the internal organisation of the force has changed remarkably little from the early years, expanding and adapting the original plan as new problems arose, rather than making fundamental changes. There are signs, however, that a period of rather greater change may be beginning. Before discussing the headquarters organisation,[2] we note briefly some facts about the Metropolitan Police District.

The M.P.D. is divided into a series of divisions in which are located the police stations. The author of a book published in 1929 wrote that the areas covered by the Metropolitan Police divisions in the central part of London had remained practically unaltered for a hundred years.[3] In the outer areas, however, where there has been the greatest growth of population, changes have been more extensive. The London Government Act, 1963, which altered the outer boundary of the Metropolitan Police District, also brought in its train the first considerable alteration in the manner of defining the boundaries of the divisions.

Under the 1963 Act,[4] the M.P.D. retained its existing area plus those parts of the new Greater London which had not previously been included, that is, Romford and Hornchurch. The total area was extended from 745 to 790 square miles. The effect is that the whole of Greater London except the City comes under the jurisdiction of the Metropolitan Police which is also responsible for policing a number of areas in Essex, Hertfordshire and Surrey.[5]

The opportunity was taken to rationalise the boundaries of the divisions. The old boundaries bore no relation to local authority boundaries; the new boundaries coincide as far as possible with the

[1] These, and other figures quoted, are taken from the Report of the Commissioner of Police of the Metropolis for the Year 1968, Cmnd. 4060, H.M.S.O., 1969.

[2] The historic name 'New Scotland Yard' was retained for the headquarters offices when the Metropolitan Police moved into new offices in Broadway in 1967, about half a mile away from the old offices.

[3] J. F. Moylan, *Scotland Yard and the Metropolitan Police*, (London, Putnam, 1929), pp. 78–9.

[4] Section 76.

[5] These include Potters Bar, Chigwell, Epsom and Ewell, Esher and Staines, among others.

boundaries of the London boroughs, thus facilitating relations between the police and the boroughs. For example, 'B' division coincides with the area of the London borough of Kensington & Chelsea and 'Q' Division covers the area of the two London boroughs of Brent and Harrow. Only in Westminster are divisions smaller, the borough area containing three whole divisions. Altogether, there are now twenty-three divisions, plus the river police (Thames Division).

Early in 1967 it was announced that a firm of management consultants had been invited 'to investigate, in the broadest possible way, the distribution of functions and responsibilities within the Metropolitan Police'.[1] It has been suggested in some quarters[2] that this move is part of a policy of bringing the M.P. more directly under Home Office control. Certainly it must be viewed in the context of the more vigorous moves in recent years towards strengthening the structure of police administration, notably by amalgamating police forces.

An extensive series of changes was introduced into the Metropolitan Police organisation from April 1, 1968, following the consultants' examination. Perhaps the most significant was the abolition of the separate Receiver's office. Although there has been no change in the Receiver's constitutional position and statutory duties, he has now become the chief administrative officer of the M.P., responsible to the Commissioner for the co-ordination of finance, supply and property management and for the efficiency of the civil staff. Simultaneously, new methods of financial control have been developed with a strengthened finance department being more closely associated with policy decisions.

The headquarters organisation now consists of ten main departments. Four, each under the control of an Assistant Commissioner, are concerned respectively with general administration, traffic, criminal investigation and personnel and training. There are three general civil-staff departments, concerned with establishment matters, finance and the administration of the Receiver's executive duties in connection with such matters as building, supplies and statistics. Finally, there are three professional departments, viz. Architect and Surveyor's, Engineering and Solicitor's. The Solicitor's department and the four under the charge of Assistant Commissioners are the responsibility of the Deputy Commissioner, the remainder of the Receiver.

Another recent change of significance followed an invitation

---

[1] *Report* of the Commissioner for 1967 (Cmnd. 3659), p. 13.
[2] e.g. *Guardian*, January 16, 1967.

to an outside research worker[1] to examine the organisation and function of the Press and Information Branch, as a result of increasing concern about relations between the police and the public. After he had made his report, a new and enlarged Public Relations Department was set up in 1967, and a Public Relations Officer appointed to be in charge of it.

There are also likely to be changes affecting the Metropolitan Police's relations with other bodies. Apart from the changes following the 1963 Act referred to above, the new responsibilities proposed for the G.L.C. in the traffic field under the 1968 White Paper[2] may lead ultimately to a redefinition of the respective roles of the police and the G.L.C. What is proposed immediately is the setting up of a Joint Traffic Executive for Greater London to co-ordinate the work of the M.P.'s Traffic and Transport Department and the G.L.C.'s Highways and Transportation Department in traffic management schemes, road safety measures and similar areas of mutual concern. It is not yet clear exactly how this joint body will operate, but it appears to be an attempt to put on a more formal basis the existing informal arrangements which have grown up to meet the changed situation since the G.L.C. assumed traffic powers in 1965. There is no suggestion at this stage that the G.L.C. has any desire to take over police powers in relation to traffic matters. Indeed the Metropolitan Police would argue that although their traffic powers are somewhat distinct from many of their other duties, they are nevertheless an integral part of the police function. It remains to be seen how effectively the new Traffic Executive will be able to co-ordinate these powers with the wide responsibilities which the G.L.C. will have.

It is not easy to sum up the advantages and disadvantages of the Metropolitan Police force. Partly by accident and partly by design it has assumed some of the characteristics of a national force. The Special Branch, for example, was set up originally as a temporary measure to meet a particular situation[3] and is now in effect a national 'political police' force.[4] The Criminal Record Office maintained by the Metropolitan Police is a central repository used by police forces all over the country. Similarly, the famous Criminal Investigation Department, which in the public mind is practically synonymous with Scotland Yard, frequently makes available to other forces on request

[1] Dr Belson, the head of the Survey Research Centre of the London School of Economics.

[2] *Transport in London* (Cmnd. 3686).

[3] On the origins of the Special Branch see Moylan, op. cit., p. 185; it was made permanent in 1886.

[4] Cf. Hart, op. cit., p. 117.

its experienced officers, particularly in murder cases. These activities of the M.P. result essentially from two factors; the sheer size and resources available to it, and its special position as the police force for the capital.

On the other hand, there are dangers in such a large organisation of a certain top-heaviness and remoteness leading to a reluctance to make necessary changes. Something of this attitude may be seen in the annual reports of the Commissioner which essentially have changed very little for years. They contain a great deal of useful and valuable information mixed in with much that is only of real interest to members of the force themselves. Analyses of the crime statistics lie side by side with reports on the police gardens competition or the engagements of the Metropolitan Police Band. And it is remarkable how much of the essential pattern of administration had until recently changed very little from Victorian times.

It is difficult to say how far this has affected the efficiency of the force since there are few reliable standards of comparison between forces. Figures such as the detection rate for crimes[1] for example have little meaning unless they can be related to the different conditions under which different police forces operate; and here London is in a class by itself as the whole history of the establishment of the Metropolitan Police illustrates. But it is significant that recently, as described above, there appears to have developed a more self-critical attitude. In his 1967 report the Commissioner has put it in this way:

'I have often wondered whether the Force was, in the era of rapid development, relying too much on self generated ideas for its progress, and whether an examination from without was required.'[2]

Whether this is the whole reason for recent developments such as the appointment of management consultants, or whether in part this reflects a greater concern on the part of the Home Secretary with the way in which the force is run, are less important in the long run than the contribution which such developments make to the increased efficiency of the Metropolitan Police. And here the signs are encouraging in the measures already proposed and put into effect, not least because they indicate a new awareness of the problems of adapting an old-established organisation to changing needs.

[1] The 'percentage of offences cleared up' was 22·3 (1966), 24·3 (1967) and 24·8 (1968). These compare with figures for the rest of the country of 45·8 (1966), 46·3 (1967) and 46·6 (1968). In both cases there are wide variations for different types of offences. (See Cmnd. 4060 and *Report* of H.M. Chief Inspector of Constabulary, 1968, H.C. 305, 1969).

[2] Cmnd. 3659, p. 13.

THE METROPOLITAN WATER BOARD

As with the police, the problems of London's water supply exercised a good deal of attention over a long period of time before an acceptable solution was found. But the solution in this case was not reached until the beginning of this century.[1] The Metropolis Water Act of 1902 established a single authority, the Metropolitan Water Board, with representatives of the local authorities in the area, to be responsible for supplying water in an area which included the whole of the county of London and a good deal of what later became the remainder of Greater London.

The arrangements for the appointment of the M.W.B. under the 1902 Act provided for sixty-six members to be appointed by the constituent authorities, plus the Lee and Thames Conservancies.[2] Although the L.C.C. always provided the largest single group of members of the Board, it was not by any means an L.C.C.-dominated body.[3]

Thus in form the M.W.B. is like any other joint board of local authorities. It differs from them in its size and scale of operations and, correspondingly, in being subject to formal and specific statutory regulation. The 1902 Act was mainly concerned with the financial arrangements involved in the assumption by the new Board of its responsibility for supplying water. Nevertheless, the statute went into some detail over the constitution of the Board. It specified the number of members to be appointed by each constituent authority; some smaller authorities were to be grouped together for the purposes of appointing a member, and the Act specified the manner in which they were to do this; the Board were to appoint a Chairman and Vice-Chairman, not necessarily from among their own members, and, interestingly, might pay them salaries; the term of office was to be three years, as for members of local authorities; and the Board could appoint committees in the same manner as a county council.[4]

The basic constitution of the Board has changed little since it first met in April 1903. There have, however, been two changes in the number of members. In 1956 the number was increased from sixty-six to eighty-eight. Then, following the London Government Act 1963, the Ministry of Housing and Local Government proposed a

[1] For the historical background, see *London's Water Supply*, 1903–1953 (Staples Press for M.W.B., 1953), Chapter 1; also W. A. Robson, *The Government and Misgovernment of London*, Chapter XI.

[2] For these two latter bodies, see below, p. 166.

[3] Fourteen of the sixty-six members were from the L.C.C. (1902 Act, Section 1(3)).

[4] Metropolis Water Act, 1902, Section 1 and Third Schedule.

large reduction in membership, no doubt having in mind the reduced number of local authorities and of councillors in Greater London as a result of the reorganisation. The Board were reluctant to accept this proposal, mainly because they thought the proposed reduction was too severe. Nevertheless, a Ministerial Order was made under which from November 1, 1965 the Board has consisted of thirty-nine members.[1]

Once it had been established the M.W.B. attracted little attention for many years.[2] It got on quietly with the job first of rationalising the system which it inherited and then increasingly as time went on of making provision for the ever-increasing needs of London for water.

There have, nevertheless, been two occasions in the last twenty years when fundamental questions have been raised about the position of the M.W.B. These questions have arisen in connection with the two related problems of the Board's area and its constitution. The statutory area of the M.W.B. as laid down in the 1902 Act bore no relation either to local authority boundaries or to the boundaries of other special authorities such as the Metropolitan Police.[3] For example, not only did the boundary of the M.W.B.'s area run through the middle of Middlesex, but it also cut through individual county districts, e.g. Hendon and Sunbury-on-Thames. Altogether the area covered 540 square miles, but there were numerous anomalies in the boundaries. At least until the reorganisation of London government in 1965 the constitution of the M.W.B. as a joint board was thus practically the only way in which the numerous local authorities included in this area could participate in the work of providing a water supply.

In 1946 a Departmental Committee was set up to examine the existing system of water supply administration in the Greater London area and to report on any changes they thought desirable. They were particularly requested to advise on the 'constitution, powers and duties' of any new body or bodies which they thought should be established. The immediate antecedent of this committee was the proposal by the Metropolitan Water Board for the establishment of a Greater London Water Area, mainly on hydro-geological

[1] Twenty-seven from the London Boroughs whose areas are wholly or partly in the M.W.B. area, including the City; six from the G.L.C.; 1 each from the Essex, Herts, Kent and Surrey C.C.s, the Thames Conservancy and the Lee Conservancy Catchment Board.

[2] There was, however, a departmental committee which in 1920 enquired into the working of the 1902 Act (Monro Committee).

[3] See Map 4 in *Report* of Royal Commission on Local Government in Greater London (Cmnd. 1164, 1960).

grounds. Under the Water Act of 1945 there was provision for a reduction in the number of water undertakings in the country and for the establishment of regional advisory bodies. In Greater London this raised particular problems partly because apart from the M.W.B., the largest water undertaking in the country, the area was supplied by a large number of undertakings large and small.[1] It was generally agreed therefore that 'the existing conglomeration of undertakings in the area must go'.[2] There was no agreement, however, on what kind of organisation of water supply would best meet the circumstances of London. The M.W.B.'s proposal for a single public representative authority for an area much larger than Greater London[3] was rejected, but the five members of the committee could not agree on an alternative; two of them favoured a small *ad hoc* appointed authority to be responsible for water supply in an area approximating to that proposed by the M.W.B.; the other three favoured four joint boards as independent supply authorities with a central water authority as a co-ordinating body.

This committee was significant chiefly for the fact that, apart from the more limited Monro Committee of 1920, it was the first enquiry specifically directed at the area and constitution of the M.W.B. since the latter had been set up in 1902, itself an indication of how effectively the board had carried out its job and in marked contrast to the numerous enquiries and proposals which had preceded the 1902 Act. The lack of agreement, however, among the committee's members was the main reason why no change was made in the position of the M.W.B. in the years following the committee's report in 1948. But in accordance with the provisions of the Water Act, 1945, the number of water undertakings elsewhere was steadily reduced, including some which served parts of the Greater London area.

This was the position when in 1957 the Minister of Housing and Local Government announced the Government's decision to establish a Royal Commission to examine local government in Greater London. As was pointed out earlier, the administration of water supply was, like that of the police, specifically excluded from the Commission's terms of reference, although the Prime Minister (Mr Macmillan) did indicate that this was 'for separate consideration'.[4] It was not clear at the time what was intended by this phrase, and it was not until after the Government had issued their White

[1] One hundred and nine undertakings in the area examined by the committee.
[2] *Report* of Departmental Committee on Greater London Water Supplies (H.M.S.O., 1948), para. 57.
[3] ibid., para. 10.
[4] H.C. Deb., November 28, 1957, cols. 1279–80.

Paper on London Government[1] that they turned their attention to the water question.

Their decision was made known in a letter from the Minister of Housing and Local Government (Dr Charles Hill) to the Board on April 4, 1962, in which he said that it had been decided to abolish the Board and transfer its functions to a committee of the proposed Greater London Council. The Board objected strongly not only to the proposal itself but also to the abrupt manner in which it had been made without detailed consultation or formal enquiry. There was, however, an obvious case for water to be a G.L.C. function, just as it had long been a municipal function in large provincial cities such as Liverpool and Leeds. One of the main objections to the L.C.C.'s taking over responsibility for water had been that it covered only a part of the area of a metropolitan water authority. The same objection could not be made to the G.L.C. It is true that the area of Greater London would not exactly coincide with that of the M.W.B., but nor would the areas in which the G.L.C. was to assume responsibility for main sewers and land drainage.

In the event, no provision was made in the London Government Act, 1963, for this transfer of the M.W.B. to the G.L.C. The reason was purely technical. Inclusion of such a provision would have made the Bill a 'Hybrid', that is, one which was of both public and private significance since it could be held that the M.W.B. was a local or private interest. In Parliamentary procedure a Hybrid Bill must go through a different and more lengthy process than the Public Bills normally introduced by Governments. In the political circumstances of 1962–3, with a General Election due in 1964 at the latest, the Government could not afford any lengthy delays if the London Government Bill was to be enacted, and preparations put in hand for the new system before the election. It was therefore announced that separate legislation would be introduced to transfer the M.W.B. to the G.L.C. This has not yet been done, although there has been no public indication that the policy of the Labour Government differs from that of its Conservative predecessor. One reason for delay may simply be pressure on the Parliamentary time-table. But another reason is almost certainly the very much bigger and more difficult transfer now proposed of the London Transport undertaking to the G.L.C. Until the problems raised by this transfer have been resolved, it is likely that Governments will continue to postpone the demise of the Metropolitan Water Board. This too is a tribute to the fact that London's water supply has for nearly seventy years been flowing smoothly under the direction of the Board.

[1] Cmnd. 1562, November 1961; on this, see above, pp. 42–44.

LONDON TRANSPORT

As with water, the setting-up of the G.L.C. has led to proposals for organisational changes in London's transport services. Rather different circumstances have, however, accompanied this latter move. Public transport services by bus and underground train in the whole of Greater London except for a small part of the London borough of Havering and a considerable area beyond are provided exclusively by the London Transport Board, a public board whose members are appointed by the Minister of Transport. This current (1969) position will be modified by proposals made in the White Paper *Transport in London* and in the Transport (London) Act, 1969.

Under the Act, the G.L.C. is to assume responsibility for London Transport, and will also come into closer relations with the other main provider of transport services in London, the British Railways Board. These proposals have come about not as the result of any outside enquiry[1] but from discussions between the various parties involved. But to see how and why they have arisen it is necessary to look first briefly at the background to the present situation.

Provision of public passenger-carrying transport in London was in private hands until the introduction of municipal tramway services in the 1890s. Apart from the main-line railway companies which already by the early years of this century had extensive suburban networks, the main ingredients of these transport services were the buses, the underground railways, and the trams. The first two came largely under the control of a private combine particularly after 1912 when the London General Omnibus Company with a 'virtual monopoly'[2] of the bus services was acquired.[3] The Chairman of the combine was Mr Albert Stanley, later Lord Ashfield. The trams were largely municipally owned, the L.C.C. having the biggest network.

During the 1920s there was considerable dissatisfaction with these arrangements and proposals for unification of the management of London's transport were put forward by, among others, the London and Home Counties Traffic Advisory Committee set up under the London Traffic Act 1924, and by Lord Ashfield and Mr Frank Pick, the General Manager of the combine. The reasons which won

[1] The Herbert Commission's terms of reference did not include passenger transport services, although they suggested that there was a problem 'worthy of study' by someone else (Cmnd. 1164, para. 440).

[2] Christopher I. Savage, *An Economic History of Transport* (London: Hutchinson, 1959), p. 128.

[3] By 1933 approximately 60 per cent of London's transport was in the hands of the combine (Ernest Davies in *Public Enterprise* (London: Allen & Unwin, 1937), p. 158).

acceptance of the idea of amalgamation are complex but have been summarised as follows:[1]

(i) the variety of competing agencies (this chiefly applied to the roads where there were a large number of small bus and coach companies set up after the First World War in competition with London General);
(ii) street congestion which was already becoming a serious problem and was aggravated by the situation described in (i);
(iii) the need for capital investment to develop the tubes or underground railways.

It was largely due to Mr Herbert Morrison (as he then was) that the solution which was eventually found was for the amalgamated undertakings to be put under the control of a public board.[2] This was the London Passenger Transport Board set up in 1933 with Lord Ashfield as chairman and Mr Pick as chief executive; it had the primary duty of securing an 'adequate and properly co-ordinated system of passenger transport for the London Passenger Transport Area'.[3] It was expected to be financially self-supporting.

The L.P.T.B. lasted until 1948. It was not the first example of a public board, but it was significant as in some ways the precursor of the bodies set up under the post-1945 nationalisation measures. With it, a unique solution had been found for a London problem but, as so often in the past, this was because London's existing governmental institutions were not suitable for running public transport. In large cities such as Birmingham, Liverpool and Manchester, municipal transport undertakings were common. In London there was no municipal authority whose area made sense for public transport purposes.

The London Passenger Transport Area covered nearly 2,000 square miles, over three times the size of Greater London; it stretched from Luton to Horsham, and from Gravesend to Windsor. It was the area within which London Transport was permitted to operate until the Transport (London) Act, 1969, became effective. Within it is a smaller area of about 1,550 square miles where London Transport had a monopoly of bus and underground services.[4]

The L.P.T.B. enjoyed a considerable measure of independence, mainly because members of the board were chosen not by the Minis-

---

[1] Savage, op. cit., p. 163.
[2] The Bill put forward in 1933 was a modified version of one originally proposed by Morrison as Minister of Transport, 1929–31.
[3] London Passenger Transport Act, 1933, Section 1.
[4] See maps in annual reports of London Transport Board.

ter of Transport but by a statutory body of appointing trustees, consisting of the Chairman of the L.C.C., the President of the Law Society, the President of the Institute of Chartered Accountants, the Chairman of the Committee of London Clearing Bankers, a member of the London and Home Counties Traffic Advisory Committee and the Chairman of the Board himself. The aim was to ensure that the choice was not subject to political influence.

Under the Transport Act, 1947, which established the British Transport Commission to be responsible for the railways and related services, the L.P.T.B. was replaced by a London Transport Executive (L.T.E.). The L.T.E., although it had the same broad sphere of powers as its predecessor, was made subordinate to the British Transport Commission. Its assets were transferred to the B.T.C. which thus assumed ultimate responsibility for the finances of the L.T.E. The Minister of Transport, however, became responsible for appointing the members of the Executive.

This was not a happy arrangement largely because London's transport problems required rather different treatment from the general problems of the railways which were the main concern of the B.T.C.[1] In 1953 the Conservative Government appointed a committee of inquiry into London Transport which concluded that 'the undertaking carried on by the London Transport Executive is conducted efficiently and with due regard to economy.'[2] They did not, however, give any positive recommendation on whether the L.T.E. should be completely separated from the B.T.C. as the old L.P.T.B. had been, or whether it should be brought more closely under the B.T.C. with the aim of bringing about closer co-ordination with British Railways services.

However, increasing concern by the Government over the future of the railways led to major changes being made under the Transport Act, 1962, to the organisation of the nationalised transport industry. As a result, the B.T.C. was abolished and its assets and functions divided among four separate public authorities, of which a newly constituted London Transport Board (L.T.B.) was one. Thus London Transport reverted very largely to the kind of organisation and powers which it had possessed under the 1933 Act. It had the same duty to provide an adequate and properly co-ordinated system of passenger transport 'with due regard to efficiency, economy and safety

[1] One critic of the arrangement has gone much further and argued that it has had the effect of subordinating 'a first-rate concern to a third-rate undertaking' (W. A. Robson, *Nationalized Industry and Public Ownership*, London, Allen & Unwin, 1960, p. 103).

[2] *Report* of the Committee of Inquiry into London Transport (Chairman S. P. Chambers), H.M.S.O., 1955, para. 391.

of operation' and the same restrictions on its activities both inside and outside the London Passenger Transport Area, for example, in relation to the hiring out of buses and coaches. Like most nationalised undertakings, it was under obligation to pay its way.

The Chairman of the Board was to be appointed by the Minister of Transport and the members by the Minister after consulting the Chairman.[1] The Board was given a specific duty to co-operate with the British Railways Board in securing proper co-ordination of L.T. and B.R. services and 'to afford to the Railways Board such information of proposed changes in their services, and such opportunities for consultation, as the Railways Board may reasonably require for that purpose.'[2] There was a reciprocal obligation on the Railways Board.

Soon, further questions were raised about the future organisation of London's public transport, partly as a result of the creation of the G.L.C. and the Labour Government's new approach to transport policies. The new Board itself also began to stress the advantages of planning land use and urban transport as part of a single, comprehensive plan.[3] But there were also particular problems of London Transport which came under examination and reopened the organisational question.

London Transport is a large undertaking, employing 69,000 staff, operating nearly 8,000 buses and over 4,000 railway carriages, collecting over £100,000,000 in fares every year, and having assets of nearly £300 million.[4] The Chambers Committee in 1955 concluded: 'London has one of the best transport systems in the world.'[5] In 1960 Professor Robson declared: 'It is not only the largest but also the best system of public transport existing in any great city of the world.'[6] Why then should there be further need to enquire into the organisation?

The answer lies basically in two related factors – the increasing difficulty in providing public transport services in a metropolitan area and the increasing difficulty of making such services pay. Several factors are important to the first point; increasingly public transport is being used simply for the journey to and from work; increased demand in peak hours has been accompanied by a decline in the demand for public transport outside the peak hours, resulting in 'a

[1] Transport Act, 1962, Section 1(4).

[2] ibid., 7(2).

[3] Cf. the article 'Moving About in Cities' by the Chairman of the London Transport Board (*The Times*, January 15, 1963).

[4] L.T.B. Annual Report and Accounts, 1968 (H.C. 208, April 22, 1969).

[5] *Report*, para. 392.

[6] W. A. Robson, op. cit., p. 101.

growing imbalance between peak and off-peak demand'[1]; at the same time increased road congestion had made it more difficult to run satisfactory bus services. On the financial side, concentration of demand into two relatively short periods each day results in an uneconomic use of plant and labour. At the same time costs, particularly labour costs, which form 70 per cent of the whole, have been rising steeply.

The facts of the situation can be briefly summarised in the following figures:[2]

passengers carried on buses and coaches declined steadily from 2,593 million in 1960 to 1,946 million in 1968, a drop of 25 per cent; passengers carried on the underground have remained fairly constant, being 674 million in 1960 and 655 million in 1968; total passengers declined by 20 per cent, from 3,267 million to 2,601 million;

although there was a sharp decline in the mileage run by buses and coaches, the cost (per car mile) rose from 38·6 pence in 1960 to 59·3 pence in 1967; for the underground the corresponding figures are 30·2 and 46·1;

working surpluses of around £8 million (i.e. before payment of interest charges) in the years 1960–62 had declined to just over £1 million in 1966 and to a deficit of £3·7 million in 1967 and £2·4 million in 1968.[3]

To the extent that London Transport was failing to pay its way, the deficit had to be met by the Exchequer, an arrangement which by 1968 the Government felt to be wrong in principle.[4] This helped to give some urgency to discussions over the future of London Transport. But the difficult underlying problem was how to reconcile the L.T.B.'s duty to provide an adequate service with its financial obligation to pay its way in the changed circumstances of the 1960s. This problem was in 1966 referred by the Minister to a Directing Group drawn largely from the Ministry of Transport and the L.T.B. with a representative of the T.G.W.U. and two outside members, under the chairmanship of Mr Stephen Swingler, then Minister of State at the Ministry.

The Group found that under existing conditions and with the

---

[1] *Transport in London* (Cmnd. 3686), p. 32.

[2] Taken from *Transport in London*, pp. 69–70, and L.T.B. *Report* for 1968, Tables S. 7 and S. 8.

[3] In both 1965 and 1967 the Government intervened to defer fare increases proposed by the L.T.B.; this was a major factor in the failure of the L.T.B. to pay its way.

[4] Cmnd. 3686, para. 7.

interpretation then being put on their obligations there was no way of reconciling the two duties of the L.T.B. Furthermore they were hampered by restrictions placed on them at a time when circumstances were different. All applications for fare increases, for example, had to go through the cumbersome procedure of the Transport Tribunal designed to safeguard the public and other interests at a time when competition from private cars was much more limited. The Group wanted to see more flexibility in the L.T.B.'s charging policies and this could not be done with the existing procedures.[1]

The Group's report is significant, however, not only for its detailed suggestions on matters such as fares policies, but also for its emphasis on the wider implications of running a public transport system in London. It recognised the need for integrated planning of all aspects of transport and traffic in London in conjunction with land-use planning; and for measures to improve L.T.B.'s competitive position which would be facilitated by such integrated planning. This wider approach has been one of the key factors in the negotiations which preceded the White Paper's proposal that the G.L.C. should assume responsibility for London Transport.

The Group's main task, however, was to suggest ways in which the L.T.B. might improve its performance (e.g. by achieving higher productivity), and, above all, to find an answer to the question of finance. Since on these points the Group's recommendations were largely followed by the White Paper, the latter's proposals so far as they affect London Transport will now be considered.

First, in place of the London Transport Board a London Transport Executive is to be set up; its members will be appointed by the G.L.C. which will stand in much the same relation to the Executive as the Minister of Transport does to the present Board (e.g. the G.L.C. will lay down general policies and be responsible for approving budgets). An important change is that the G.L.C. will take over responsibility for fares policies.[2]

Secondly, the new L.T.E. will be responsible for most public transport in the Greater London area. So far as buses are concerned, the central or red buses will be transferred in their entirety from the L.T.B. to the L.T.E.; the country or green buses which mostly operate outside Greater London and the long-distance Green Line coaches will go to the new National Bus Company. The underground system is being transferred as a whole to the L.T.E. even though some of its routes run beyond Greater London, e.g. to Epping.

[1] The report of the Directing Group is printed as an Annex to the 1968 White Paper (Cmnd. 3686, pp. 27–85).
[2] Cmnd. 3686, paras. 46, 47.

The London Passenger Transport Area which has existed since 1933 will disappear.[1]

Thirdly, the White Paper is less specific on the financial terms of the take-over. This is understandable in view of the fact that the G.L.C.'s agreement to the new arrangements is very much conditioned by the financial terms which are therefore the subject of some hard bargaining. From this point of view, perhaps the most important proposal in the White Paper is that 90 cer cent of the L.T.B.'s capital debt should be written off, the remainder to be assumed partly by the G.L.C. and partly by the National Bus Company. From the day when the G.L.C. assumes responsibility there will of course be no question of Exchequer subsidy and any deficit will have to be met by the ratepayers of Greater London. Hence it is understandable that the G.L.C. was anxious that London Transport should be solvent at the time of takeover and that the financial arrangements should at least offer a chance of maintaining that solvency. The G.L.C.'s power to determine the structure and general level of fares is therefore of particular importance.[2]

Finally, there is the important question of statutory duties and objectives to which the Directing Group had devoted much attention. The White Paper here proposes two tasks to replace the present ones laid down in the 1962 Act. First, the L.T.E. is to 'provide or secure the provision of public passenger transport services which, in conjunction with those of B.R. and the N.B.C., best meet the current needs of London as interpreted from time to time by the G.L.C.' Secondly, the Executive will have to meet financial objectives agreed in advance with the G.L.C. and covering a defined period.[3] In other words, it will be entirely up to the G.L.C. to decide what kind of transport system it wants in Greater London. This will be the first time in its history that the capital has had this power. The power will, however, be subject to the important exception that the main-line railways which carry the bulk of suburban commuters will still operate independently of the G.L.C. It is true that a closer working relationship with British Railways is envisaged in the White Paper, but its terms are somewhat vague, and it remains to be seen whether it leads to more effective integration of B.R. and L.T. services.

A great deal remains to be done before G.L.C. control of London Transport becomes a reality. No date has yet been fixed for the transfer. An urgent question for the G.L.C. meanwhile is how to adapt its organisation to these new responsibilities. In the revised committee

[1] ibid., para. 48.
[2] ibid., paras. 50, 54. See also Transport (London) Amendment Act, 1969.
[3] ibid., para. 52.

structure adopted in July 1968, arrangements for control of London's transport system were assigned to the Policy Steering Committee whose main concern is with medium- and long-term objectives for all the council's services. But a great deal will turn on how effectively transport planning is made part of the G.L.C.'s comprehensive planning. This calls for strong efforts in co-ordination so that the needs of public transport are given due weight.

Again, the practical as opposed to the formal relationship between the G.L.C. and the Executive will be important. In theory, the G.L.C. will be responsible for general policy and the L.T.E. for day-to-day operation. It is well known that there is no firm line to be drawn between the two. Nevertheless, there must be a basic working relationship which recognises a distinction between matters which are appropriate for political decision and matters which can and should be left to the Executive.

For the G.L.C. there may be a further dilemma; if they recruit to the Executive men of the calibre they need to run this important undertaking, can they ensure that policy considerations prevail when, as must inevitably happen, there is a conflict between the views of the G.L.C. and of the Executive? There is the danger that able men may find the G.L.C.'s control irksome in just those areas of policy decision, e.g. financial objectives, where the G.L.C. may be most anxious to insist on its view. It must be remembered here that there is no precedent for a board of this kind being appointed and responsible to a local authority, even though in this case the local authority is of an unusual kind. But apart from this unusual factor, difficulties have arisen in the case of other nationalised undertakings in the relations between boards and Ministries

These potential difficulties and dangers have to be set against the potential advantages of the new arrangements. These are undoubtedly great. With land-use planning, traffic and public transport (the railways being an important exception) under one roof the potential for a determined attack on some of London's biggest problems are obvious.

Three other bodies ought to be briefly mentioned in this survey of special authorities.

THE PORT OF LONDON AUTHORITY

This was set up in 1908, largely on the model of the Mersey Docks and Harbour Board, to bring some order into the chaotic management and finances of London's docks.[1] To some extent it is thus

[1] For the history of the P.L.A. see the essay by Lincoln Gordon in *Public Enterprise*, p. 17.

parallel with the establishment of the Metropolitan Water Board in 1902. The constitution of the P.L.A. is however quite different. It consists at present of a chairman, Vice-Chairman and fourteen members, all of whom are appointed by the Minister of Transport after consultation with port interests. These include the Chamber of Shipping of the U.K. and the London General Shipowners Society, the London Wharfingers Association and the trade unions. The G.L.C., the City of London and the National Ports Council are also represented. Effectively, therefore, the P.L.A. is an indirectly elected body with representatives of port interests and local authorities. It is a public, non-profit-making body; its revenues come from dues and charges levied on goods and vessels entering the port and the docks, and it raises capital in the open market. Its main duties are the administration and improvement of London's docks, the conservancy of the river Thames from Teddington Lock to the sea, and certain licensing powers, e.g. of river craft and lightermen.[1] The P.L.A. has always been a vigorous and active body: a recent illustration has been the building of a vast new container port at Tilbury. Correspondingly, some of the older docks nearer the city are being run down (e.g. St Katharine and London docks).

THAMES CONSERVANCY

Officially, they are the conservators of the river Thames and were first appointed in 1857 with jurisdiction from Staines to the sea (extended to Cricklade in 1866). Their powers below Teddington Lock were transferred to the P.L.A. by the 1908 Act and therefore their jurisdiction now covers only a very small part of Greater London.

LEE CONSERVANCY CATCHMENT BOARD

The Board is the land drainage and flood prevention authority in the Lee catchment area, exercising powers which elsewhere are performed by river authorities and by the G.L.C. It is also responsible for the prevention of pollution. In constitution it is a joint board of the local authorities in its area, on which it precepts. The M.W.B. is also represented and contributes to the Board's finances for work on prevention of pollution.

[1] Also licensing of port employers under the Dock and Harbours Act, 1966.

Chapter VIII

CONCLUSION

A major theme of the preceding chapters has been that London government has always provided special problems, and that the London Government Act of 1963 was an important attempt to devise a structure which would meet those problems. It was furthermore a wide-ranging measure, unlike earlier legislation such as the Metropolis Management Act of 1855 or even the Local Government Act of 1888 which dealt with only a part of London's government. Even so, as the projected transfers of London Transport and the Metropolitan Water Board indicate, the 1963 Act left some parts of London government untouched. If these transfers to the G.L.C. are successfully carried through, directly elected authorities covering an area of 620 square miles with a population of nearly eight million people will be responsible for all the important local services with the notable exception of the police.

Nothing on this scale exists in local government anywhere else in the country. Nor has there yet been a reorganisation of areas, functions and status on the scale which followed the London Government Act, 1963, since the modern local government system was established in the late nineteenth century. That is why so much attention has been devoted in these pages to analysing the background to the 1963 reforms and to describing the new structure and how it came into being.

Three major questions suggested by the London government reforms will be examined here: first, how the new system is working; secondly, whether the areas and constitution of the new authorities are the right ones; thirdly, what are the wider implications of the London reforms.

THE WORKING OF THE NEW SYSTEM

This is a formidable question to answer. It is concerned not only with the effect which the reforms have had on the performance of services but also with the working of the new authorities as democratic institutions.

Performance of functions

The new system of London government has been in existence only a few years. This is too short a time for it to be possible to make final judgments on its effectiveness. It must be remembered that even with such a large reorganisation as that carried out under the 1963 Act there was not a complete break with the past. Most of the members and officers of the new authorities, for example, had served under the old system. They might be faced with new responsibilities and duties, but they were bound to carry over to the new system ideas and attitudes which they had grown used to under the old, and which might or might not be appropriate to the new situation. But it seems desirable to emphasise this element of continuity in the early years of the new system.

Again, it has been stressed how formidable was the job of making the transition from the old to the new system. It is not surprising, therefore, that preoccupation with getting the services organised on the new basis should in many cases have continued well beyond April 1, 1965. Furthermore, a number of difficulties are likely to face the new authorities for some time. There is, for example, the problem facing the London boroughs of provision of adequate office and other accommodation for their staffs; with the amalgamation of anything up to five of the old authorities to form a new London borough, the difficulties of siting offices have often been great, and these difficulties have a bearing on the efficient performance of services.

Given then, that the time may not be ripe for a final verdict on the new system, it may nevertheless be possible to assess its potentialities for the performance of functions and to identify tendencies which are appearing. In attempting to do this we have very much in mind the view of the Herbert Commission that under the old system some functions were either not being performed at all or at least not being performed satisfactorily. One of the main justifications for changing the system, therefore, was to provide a structure which would enable these functions to be performed satisfactorily. At the same time, we have to keep in mind the views of opponents of the Commission's proposals and, later, of the Government's plan, that a change would lead to a less satisfactory performance of some services.

An examination in detail of the whole range of services provided by the G.L.C. and the boroughs would be a very large undertaking.[1]

[1] The Greater London Group of the London School of Economics and Political Science is at present engaged on a large-scale study examining the effects of the reforms on the major local government services in Greater London; this is not likely to be published before 1971.

In Chapters V and VI we examined some of the services which seemed to us most critical to an assessment of the working of the present system of local government in Greater London. In the following pages we draw on those chapters and refer briefly to other services, under three categories: (i) services provided exclusively by the G.L.C.; (ii) services provided jointly by the G.L.C. and the boroughs; (iii) services provided exclusively by the boroughs.

(i) *G.L.C. services.* There are not many services provided only by the G.L.C., and of those which are, some are of a relatively minor nature, such as the organisation of the *Coroners' service* and the provision of coroners' courts. There are other services, such as *traffic management*, for which the G.L.C. is responsible but which are so closely connected with other services shared with the boroughs that they are best considered under that heading.

The *ambulance* and *fire services* are probably the most important under this heading. Of all the services transferred to the G.L.C. these aroused least controversy, even opponents of the 1963 Act acknowledging that if there was to be a G.L.C. it was right that it should have responsibility for these services. All the indications are that this has proved a successful transfer and that when the process of rationalisation and integration is complete these services will be seen to have benefited from the new system.

Mention should also be made here of the G.L.C.'s *Research and Intelligence Unit* which, although not exclusively serving the G.L.C., is an example of the kind of service which the G.L.C. is in a good position to provide for the benefit of Greater London as a whole. Somewhat similar, though more limited in scope, is the G.L.C.'s *Scientific Branch*, which it inherited from the L.C.C.

(ii) *G.L.C./borough services.* These cover a wide range from planning to sewerage, and from housing to land drainage. Two major services in this category which have not been considered in earlier chapters are housing and education.

In *housing*, perhaps the main questions are what should be the role of the G.L.C., and how effective have the boroughs been in providing for London's housing needs. There is general agreement that the G.L.C. has a significant role to play and that it needs to retain access to a fairly large amount of accommodation if it is to fulfil this strategic role of balancing the needs of the different areas of Greater London.[1] It can do this within Greater London partly by retaining or continuing to build its own houses, the tenancies of which can be allocated to those with the most pressing housing needs; and partly by securing agreements with the more favourably

[1] See *The Housing Role of the Greater London Council within London* (Report of Standing Working Party on London Housing, H.M.S.O., 1967).

situated boroughs to nominate tenants to a proportion of their housing. Behind these arrangements lies the dominant fact of London's housing situation that the worst problems are concentrated in a relatively few areas of inner London in such boroughs as Southwark, Islington and Tower Hamlets, and that not enough land is available in these boroughs for them to be able to solve their problems on their own. On the other hand, many of the outer boroughs have comparatively small housing problems and are not so desperately short of land for building.

The G.L.C. has had a fair amount of success in securing nomination agreements with many of the outer London boroughs, usually on the basis that the G.L.C. should be able to nominate tenants to a proportion (often 10 per cent) of the new houses built by the borough. At the same time, the G.L.C. still retains the temporary powers inherited from the L.C.C. of being able to build anywhere within Greater London, and is currently building about 6,000 houses a year. When these powers are finally terminated the G.L.C. will only be able to build with borough consent for most purposes. It remains, therefore, an open question whether in the long run the G.L.C. will be able to secure sufficient agreements with the outer boroughs to enable it to continue to play an effective role in meeting the needs of the most hard-pressed areas. The problem will be accentuated when the transfers of G.L.C. housing to the boroughs get under way.[1] Under proposals made in 1969, 71,000 houses were to be transferred to the boroughs in 1970, although the G.L.C. was to retain nomination rights to a large proportion of them.[2]

Outside Greater London only the G.L.C. is empowered to make arrangements, under the Town Development Act, 1952, with other authorities for the expansion of existing towns to take population from London. In this sphere the G.L.C. seems to have done little more than carry on schemes already operated or planned by the L.C.C. The largest new scheme was concluded with Hastings in 1969 to provide 3,500 houses for Londoners. The situation may be partly due to the difficulty of finding suitable towns for expansion since the G.L.C., like the L.C.C., has never tried to force a scheme on an unwilling partner; partly, it may be because these schemes have tended to be overshadowed by the much larger projects initiated by the Government, particularly the New Town at Milton Keynes in Buckinghamshire, and the large expansion schemes at Northampton and Peterborough.

[1] London Government Act, 1963, Section 23(4).
[2] Up to 65 per cent: two boroughs, however, with large allocations totalling 12,000 houses (Hackney and Tower Hamlets) have refused to accept the transfer.

It is difficult to assess how successfully the boroughs are tackling their housing problems. There has been a considerable increase in building programmes in the first few years of the new authorities' existence. Much of this was, however, planned by the old authorities before the new system came into operation. Moreover, the Labour Government in 1964 took the initiative in pressing for an increase in London's housing programme, helped by the publication early in 1965 of the Milner Holland Report[1] which drew attention to the still considerable problems existing in some parts of London. On the kind of issue where one would have hoped for improvements under the new system, such as the rationalisation of rent structures throughout Greater London, little has been done. Perhaps the main impression at the moment is that the reforms themselves have not so far made a great deal of impact on the housing position, but the next few years should show whether the potentialities of the new system are being realised, and, in particular, whether the G.L.C. is able to achieve an effective strategic role.

In *education* even more than in housing there is need for a detailed enquiry into the working of the new system,[2] not least because there are now two entirely different systems of administration within Greater London, the Inner London Education Authority being responsible for education in the area of the twelve inner London boroughs whereas each of the twenty outer boroughs is an education authority on its own. It is not self-evident that this dual arrangement is the right solution of the admittedly difficult problem of providing education services in a large metropolitan area. From this point of view it is a pity that the review of the working of the Inner London Education Authority which, under the 1963 Act, was to have taken place before 1970, has now been abandoned.[3] It is true that there was some dispute whether the review would have been confined simply to the question of whether the boroughs in inner London should be given some share in the education service, but on educational grounds there is a clear case for re-examining the composite arrangements in Greater London.

Not least is this true because currently there is considerable dispute about the optimum size of an education authority. In evidence to the Redcliffe-Maud Commission, the Department of Education

[1] *Report* of the Committee on Housing in Greater London (Cmnd. 2605, H.M.S.O., 1965).

[2] For information on education in Greater London, see the forthcoming volume on the local education services in the 'New Town and County Hall' series, by Mr D. E. Regan.

[3] Local Government (Termination of Reviews) Act, 1967, Section 2 (above, p. 60).

and Science suggested that there should be no more than about forty education authorities in the whole of England outside Greater London. The implication could certainly be drawn from their evidence that they thought that London with the I.L.E.A. plus twenty borough L.E.A.s had too many authorities; this view was strongly disputed by the London Boroughs' Association which claimed that the new system under the 1963 Act was working very well in outer London.[1]

The available statistics do not throw much light on this question. The following, for example, are comparative costs of education taken from the publications of the Institute of Municipal Treasurers and Accountants:

EDUCATION COSTS PER 1,000 POPULATION (£)

		A	B	C	D	E	Total	% increase
10 C.B.s	1963–4	617	5771	6962	2845	589	19,537	34
	1966–7	784	7173	8899	4572	778	26,220	
London C.C.	1963–4	876	5245	7159	3399	899	22,006	
I.L.E.A.	1966–7	1541	6623	9218	6076	1182	28,129	28
Middx. C.C.	1963–4	739	5024	7077	3522	564	19,765	
Middx. B.	1966–7	996	6317	8435	5633	706	25,903	31

A = Administration and Inspection; B = Primary Education; C = Secondary; D = Further; E = Special. For the authorities included see above, p. 132.

Administration and inspection costs have increased in the areas corresponding to the old county of Middlesex more than they have in the county boroughs outside London (35 per cent against 27 per cent); on the other hand, further education costs have gone up by 68 per cent in the county boroughs and only 60 per cent in Middlesex, against 79 per cent in the I.L.E.A. Facts such as these are the starting-point of investigation; in themselves they tell us little about the performance of authorities, which must be related among other things to the problems which different authorities have to face and to the policies which they decide to follow. Nor must it be forgotten that the Herbert Commission laid great stress on the desirability of the local element in education, both because it would attract able councillors and because it was important that parents and other members of the public should be able to have a say in how education services were provided.[2] Perhaps in education even more than in

[1] Royal Commission on Local Government in England, *Written Evidence* of Department of Education and Science, pp. 70, 111–13: London Boroughs' Association, Additional Memorandum of Evidence (April 1967), pp. 9–11.

[2] See the Commission *Report*, para. 518.

most services the antithesis between functional efficiency and the needs of local democracy are very evident. The enthusiasm of the outer London boroughs, and particularly of their Chief Education Officers, for the new system there is a healthy sign; but at the same time one must look carefully at the criticisms of those who lay stress on the ability of larger authorities to do more from their own resources, providing, for example, a greater range of specialised staff, institutions and equipment. In education caution about the working of the new system is the only reasonable attitude until a deeper investigation is possible.

In *planning*, under which we can now include the planning of land use, the road network and public transport, the G.L.C. must be the major partner if the rationale of the London reforms is to be realised in practice. There are important local issues which it is right that the boroughs should be able to represent, and represent effectively. But in the long term the success or failure of the G.L.C. will turn on whether it is able to demonstrate that its planning is creating the right environment within which London can continue to function as a city. It is an immense task, requiring the ability not only to look ahead and make plans but also to ensure that in dealing with the many conflicting claims and interests which are bound to arise, the main objectives are not lost sight of. Above all, there is a need to try to ensure that any plans have a sufficient measure of public support to be acceptable to the people who will have to live and work in the London which results from them.

The written statement of the Greater London Development Plan, published in 1969, is an indication that a satisfactory answer has not yet been found to the problem of strategic planning in Greater London. The tentative nature of that document may be to some extent justified by the relatively short time within which it had to be produced, and by the lack of reliable data on a number of matters. It is also true that the G.L.D.P. has to be seen as part of a more comprehensive approach to planning in the south-east, as exemplified by *A Strategy for the South East*.[1] Nevertheless, it remains true that the draft statement does not adequately indicate what kind of a city the Greater London of the future is likely to be; nor does it bring together the various separate strands and policies, e.g. on residential densities or environmental areas, into a coherent unified policy. Time has undoubtedly been a limiting factor, but the statement raises more fundamental questions.

[1] The first report of the South East Economic Planning Council (H.M.S.O., 1967): at the time the draft statement was produced this report was still under examination by the Government.

There is a danger that the shape of the London of the future will be determined more by what the thirty-two boroughs (and the City) individually plan with their eyes on their own areas than by the G.L.C.'s view of what is needed for London as a whole. This seems to be the implication of the G.L.D.P. draft statement. It results partly from the 1963 Act's provisions which made the boroughs plan-making authorities and did not give the G.L.C. sufficient powers to make its strategic role effective. But it also results from the G.L.C.'s seeming unwillingness to assert itself and its extreme readiness to be conciliatory towards the boroughs. It may be that from this dialogue between the G.L.C. and the boroughs there will emerge a coherent plan for London, but it is probably more likely that we shall see a compromise between conflicting interests which in the end will satisfy hardly anyone. This is one of the most critical parts of the new system, and much now depends on what reaction the boroughs make to the G.L.D.P. and how far-sightedly they use the opportunity open to them to plan for the future. But unless the G.L.C. decides to take a more positive role, it is difficult not to feel that the potentialities of the new system are unlikely to be realised.

In *traffic management*, there has been a great deal of activity since the G.L.C. was instituted. But here it is essential to distinguish short-term from long-term measures. Traffic schemes which create one-way streets and similar effects are on the whole short-term means aimed at getting the traffic to flow smoothly. Many such schemes have been introduced since 1965, but all except the most recent were largely planned before the G.L.C. was in existence. What has happened is that the G.L.C. is now responsible for introducing these schemes after consulting the boroughs and the Metropolitan Police whereas previously they were the responsibility of the Ministry of Transport. It is an advantage of the new system that inevitable conflicts of interest between traffic needs and local amentiy can now be resolved within the democratic framework of elected local authorities. If this sometimes means that measures are not introduced as quickly as the traffic experts would like, this is the inevitable and necessary price which must be paid if democratic local government is to have any meaning.

In the long term, the problem is to evolve a policy for dealing with London's traffic. Such a policy must be concerned not only with traffic management in the narrow sense, and not even with more general issues such as a parking policy. It must really be concerned with the question 'how far can or should London go in attempting to meet the problems caused by motor traffic?' We are thus brought back to the G.L.C.'s strategic role, and to the highly controversial issues raised by proposals such as that for the Motorway Box. Basically, the philosophy behind this proposal is that by making it possible for traffic to move smoothly without having to pass through the centre of London, it will be possible to evolve a better and more acceptable policy for the centre where, as is generally agreed, traffic at present causes the most acute problems. Whether the G.L.C. is evolving the right policies is a matter for argument. The important point for the present analysis is that the potentiality now exists for an authority to evolve consistent and balanced policies which take into account the whole range of issues comprised in land-use and transportation planning.

Less needs to be said about other functions, both because they tend to be less controversial and because they do not provide the essential case for the new system. Nevertheless, it is worth noting that there are indications that the new system will lead to the advantages which can be expected from large-scale organisation. This is particularly true of *sewerage and sewage disposal*, and *refuse collection and disposal*. In the latter, for example, the G.L.C.'s responsibility for refuse disposal is producing a rationalised and more effective system symbolised in the building (at a cost of £10 million) of a new refuse incineration plant which will supersede the individual and somewhat haphazard arrangements which existed previously.[1] The division of *parks and open spaces* between the G.L.C. and the boroughs has brought certain difficulties. Consultations were begun in 1968 between them to decide which of the parks which the G.L.C. had acquired from the L.C.C. should be transferred to the boroughs. The Conservative majority on the G.L.C. has seemed anxious to transfer as many as possible to the boroughs, mainly in fulfilment of the election pledge in 1967 that, in return for increased powers in the traffic field, the G.L.C. would be willing to let the boroughs have more power in other fields. The boroughs seem to be divided on this issue. Apart from the fact that large open spaces such as Hampstead Heath seem likely in any case to remain a G.L.C. responsibility, some boroughs have not been anxious to take on the increased responsibility and cost of parks which they feel in some cases at least serve much wider needs than those of their own inhabitants.

(*iii*) *Borough services*. Much the most important of the new functions of the London boroughs were those taken over from the *health, welfare and children's* departments of the former county and county borough councils.

As long ago as 1947, Aneurin Bevan, in introducing the National Assistance Bill, said: 'where the individual is concerned, where

[1] See *Report* of Herbert Commission, paras. 635–58.

humanity and warmth is the primary consideration, there the authority which is responsible should be as near the recipient as possible.'[1]

Clearly the recipient is much nearer the authority in the London boroughs than he was in the counties. In the County of London before the reforms, there was one Welfare Committee for the whole county. Now there are a dozen whose members can take a personal interest in the welfare of those in special need. There was one head office, and only three sub-offices where those requiring help could make personal application. Now there are a dozen head offices and numerous sub-offices.

Some of the figures given earlier in Chapter VI, more especially those referring to the physically handicapped, indicate the attitude to this new situation. The growing response to essentially local needs has also been shown. There were many boroughs in London which had no old people's home within their boundaries, which meant that many of the aged were removed long distances from relatives and their familiar environment. Now there is not a borough which has not planned for homes of its own, and many have already provided them.

The same applies to temporary accommodation for the homeless. Many boroughs have already produced their own small units and practically all are planning to do so. This means that children's education will not be disturbed to the same extent and men in work will not have the same difficulties over travel.

Many of these considerations apply also to health and children's departments. Moreover there is clear evidence of a much closer relationship between the three departments and with housing than there was in the counties. Finally, there is clear evidence of a keenness to pioneer and experiment and to follow up the experiments and pioneering efforts of others.

With regard to the financial effects of the reforms, there was apprehension that the multiplication of authorities might lead to a heavy increase in cost. Increase there has certainly been, but it does not appear to have been appreciably greater than that of comparable authorities elsewhere in the country.

There is less evidence of developments in children's departments, but these departments have had to face exceptional difficulties in staff recruitment. This is a direct result of the reforms, and must, therefore, be regarded to their disadvantage, but should be remedied by the passage of time.

With regard to those services operated by the former second-tier

[1] H.C. Deb. November 24, 1947, col. 1610.

authorities, the result in each borough has in general terms been to raise the standard throughout the area to the highest attained by any of the constituent authorities. In addition, the greater resources of the new boroughs has enabled them to effect economies by greater use of mechanisation, and has facilitated a better coverage.

The electors and the elected
From the analysis presented in Chapter IV it seems clear that no firm conclusions can be drawn from the voting figures of the G.L.C. and borough elections of the impact which the new system has had on the electorate. It is doubtful or at least unproven whether the Herbert Commission were right in supposing that elimination of the complications in the local government system in Greater London would contribute to the health of local government.[1] In particular, the evident tendency for voting to follow the national political fortunes of the parties, rather than to reflect the local standing of the parties on the council, makes it difficult to interpret voting figures as an indication of how Londoners view the new system.

Furthermore, there are some interesting features of the voting figures which require further study. Why, for example, should the G.L.C. elections produce higher turnouts in outer than in inner London? More research is certainly needed into the attitudes of voters, and into the whole question of whether the new system of local government has contributed anything to greater public interest in and knowledge of the affairs of their local councils.[2]

Nor, in spite of the concern of the G.L.C. and the boroughs with developing adequate public relations, is there much indication yet that their efforts are meeting with a great deal of success. At a time when 'public participation' has become a catch-phrase there is clearly an urgent need to find means of engaging the attention of members of the public in the capital in local government. It is a problem which is not of course confined to London, but it may be that it presents special difficulties there.

Finally, a great deal remains to be done in examining the effects of the new system in attracting able men and women to serve as councillors on the new authorities. The Herbert Commission laid stress on the fact that there was difficulty under the old system in attracting sufficient able councillors for the boroughs and urban districts.[3] One aim of a reorganised system was to create boroughs

---

[1] See the Commission's *Report*, especially para. 689.
[2] Some information will be available in a forthcoming study of the G.L.C. elections of 1964 and 1967 by Mr L. J. Sharpe and Dr Dilys Hill.
[3] *Report*, para. 688.

M

which would attract able people to serve on them. It is not easy to say whether this has been achieved, partly because in the elections of 1964 most of those who were elected had previously served on the old authorities, partly because the concept of what constitutes an able councillor is still somewhat elusive in spite of the work of the Herbert Commission and of the later Maud Committee on Management of Local Government.

The boroughs seem in general to be proving effective units of local government for the tasks which they have been given. The extent to which they have developed close relationships among themselves has been one of the most interesting features of the new system. Critics might claim that this is merely to conceal deficiencies in the system, and that it was unnecessary under the previous system when, for example, there were only nine authorities exercising child-care functions in the Greater London area. It is, however, one of the most difficult questions affecting local government structure to reconcile functional claims with the ability to respond to local needs. The one frequently pulls in the direction of larger and the other in the direction of smaller authorities. The London boroughs may not be the ideal size, but they have gone a good way to reconciling these differing needs; and the activities of the London Boroughs Association have played no small part in this.

Many formidable difficulties remain. Some concern the G.L.C.'s role; some the mutual relationships between the G.L.C. and the boroughs. It will take time to see whether the new system not only produces answers to London's problems but does so with due regard to the many interests which are concerned. It would be surprising if the new structure of local government had produced just the right balance of resources and powers. And just as the Herbert Commission argued that changes in the administrative structure would not by themselves ensure that London's problems would be solved, so failure to solve London's problems would not in itself indicate that the structure was wrong. On the whole, and with the reservations which have been indicated, the resources and powers exist for the G.L.C. and the boroughs to undertake the services which have been assigned to them. Beyond that, it is a question of how the powers are used.

THE CONSTITUTION AND AREAS OF THE NEW AUTHORITIES

The distinctiveness of the Greater London Council consists partly in the area which it covers, and partly in its unique powers. By contrast, the boroughs are much more akin to authorities existing elsewhere in the country; they are of a similar size to medium-to-large county boroughs,[1] but differ from the latter in having a more restricted range of powers. Their distinctiveness consists much more in their situation; they are authorities of equal status and not too dissimilar size, each forming a part of a continuous built-up area and standing in a certain relationship to the G.L.C.—an authority with powers extending over the whole of that area.

The main questions which arise in considering the new system as a whole are as follows: First, is the Greater London defined in the 1963 Act a unity and a suitable area for the performance of local government functions? Secondly, are the areas, constitution and functions of the authoritities which have been set up in Greater London appropriate?

The Herbert Commission asserted:

'there is an entity which is so closely knit, so interdependent, so deeply influenced by the central area and so largely built up, that it truly makes up the London of today. We also accept the view, put to us and established by a number of students, that the influence of London extends far beyond the Review Area.'[2]

There are therefore two arguments about the area of Greater London. The major argument is whether the Commission, followed by the Government, was right to insist on the unity of the built-up area in spite of the recognition that London's influence reached much further. The minor argument is whether, assuming that Greater London is a unity, the right boundaries were chosen to define it.

Geographers and planners have distinguished a Metropolitan Region, extending roughly to a radius of forty miles from Charing Cross.[3] Within this area live approximately 13 million people, over one-quarter of the population of England and Wales. It is an area rather bigger than that of Professor Abercrombie's Greater London Plan of 1944,[4] and it represents roughly the limits of London's influence at present, e.g. as indicated by the number and proportion of the working population in the area who commute to London.

[1] Lambeth, the largest in population of the London boroughs, has approximately the same population as Coventry, and is bigger than Nottingham or Bradford; Kingston upon Thames, the smallest, has about the same population as Birkenhead or Bournemouth.

[2] Report, paras. 895–6.

[3] See Map in *A Strategy for the South East* (Report of the South East Economic Planning Council, H.M.S.O., 1967) for the boundaries of this area and its relationship to Greater London and the South East Region.

[4] See above, p. 24.

Could this area form a London City Region and a more suitable area for strategic planning functions?

There are attractions from a planning point of view, especially if one is thinking in terms of economic as well as physical planning, in treating the Metropolitan Region as a whole. London does not stop at the Green Belt if one is thinking of the future employment and housing pattern, or of the road and railway network which will be required. It may be that there should be some body charged with the duty of preparing a plan for this area. At the moment, advice on economic planning is the function of the South East Economic Planning Council, an appointed body with no executive powers, whose area is bigger than the Metropolitan Region. Land-use planning is the responsibility of the G.L.C. and the counties and county boroughs in the South East, who meet regularly in the Standing Conference for London and South East Regional Planning to discuss and, if possible, concert their views on the overall problems of the Region.

The present pattern of local authorities in south-east England, and correspondingly the arrangements for land-use planning, may well be changed as a result of the recommendations of the Redcliffe-Maud Commission.[1] But even without judging whether the present arrangements are the most satisfactory which can be devised, one may still consider whether the wider questions of planning for the Metropolitan Region or the whole of the south-east necessarily imply that it does not make sense to have an authority for the urban centre of the region represented by Greater London. In the first place, there are some problems which differ in degree if not in kind in the urban centre. Traffic problems, for example, are particularly acute in the built-up area and especially in central London; again, the planning problems presented by the dense concentration of housing, commerce and industry are very different from those of the mixed urban and rural areas typical of most of the Metropolitan region outside Greater London; and again, the uniqueness of central London presents its own special problems.

Secondly, there is the sheer size of the task which has to be done in London; it is arguable that if the problems of planning and transportation in the urban area are to be successfully overcome, there is a need for an authority which can concentrate on just these problems.

This is not to deny the obvious fact that many of London's problems cannot be looked at in isolation. To plan for the built-up area without regard to the effect on the remainder of the south-east is no more sensible than to plan for the south-east without regard to the

[1] See *Report* of Royal Commission on Local Government in England, 1966–69 (Cmnd. 4040); its terms of reference excluded Greater London.

rest of the country. It is simply to state that there is nevertheless a reasonable argument for having a strong planning authority concerned with the urban area of London. It may be that if changes are made in the structure of local government in the remainder of the south-east, or if, for example, some body were set up to be responsible for producing a plan for the south-east, there would be a need to redefine the responsibilities of the G.L.C. in the light of the new situation. But that there would still be a need for an authority which could comprehend and take action on the problems of Greater London seems evident.

The present boundaries of Greater London, however, are not entirely appropriate. Ideally, boundaries should be defined in terms of specified criteria, but such boundaries will rarely coincide with existing local-authority boundaries. For practical reasons, therefore, quite apart from the desirability of having some regard to history and tradition, it is usually easier when creating new authorities to form them by amalgamating existing units. This was done in the case of the G.L.C., whose boundary, except in the case of the small part of Chigwell incorporated into Greater London, follows the boundaries of previous authorities.[1]

The main principle on which this was done was to take the inner edge of the Green Belt as marking the limit of the continuous built-up area. This did not give a clear-cut boundary since a number of authorities contained both urban and Green Belt parts and there was therefore room for argument about where the boundary should run. The Herbert Commission examined the position for each authority; their conclusions were not, however, accepted by the Government in every case. A more recent examination of the data, and particularly of data from the 1961 Census which were not available when the boundary decisions were taken in 1962, indicates that there are good grounds for adding all the areas suggested by the Commission but rejected by the Government, with the possible exception of Walton and Weybridge; there may be grounds for adding some additional areas such as Potters Bar and Brentwood.[2] If the Herbert Commission proposals were incorporated, adjustments would need to be made to the borough boundaries within Greater London[3] but there

[1] Not, of course, county boundaries (except for the western boundary of Middlesex), but county district boundaries.

[2] See Royal Commission on Local Government in England, Research Study I, *Local Government in South East England* by the Greater London Group (H.M.S.O. 1968), pp. 428–32.

[3] On this see Royal Commission on Local Government in England, Research Study 2, *The Lessons of the London Government Reforms* by the Greater London Group (H.M.S.O., 1968), p. 1.

would result a more logical boundary for Greater London itself.

The areas of the boroughs must be regarded as primarily areas of administrative convenience. Within the boundaries of Greater London the Government aimed to create authorities of at least 200,000 population by amalgamation of existing authorities. Given these over-riding constraints, an attempt was made to create unions which had some coherence, e.g. because they were linked by lines of communication. But inevitably some of the borough groupings seemed to be of authorities with little in common; an example is Wembley and Willesden which now form the London borough of Brent.

This is not necessarily a situation to be deplored. A search for communities in London beyond the very localised level of places like Blackheath or Dulwich or Camden Town might not be very rewarding, and these places are too small in themselves to serve as major local authorities. Perhaps of more importance in London is whether the London boroughs are the right kind of areas for providing the services for which they are responsible. This is not simply a question of ability in terms of resources to provide an adequate standard, as was discussed above. It is obviously important that the boroughs should not be too large if they are to fulfil their purpose of providing local services, giving people access to those who provide the services and allowing members of the council to keep in touch with the needs of those whom they represent. It is probable that if boroughs were much larger, they would have less advantages over their predecessors in this respect than has been noted earlier. This is particularly true of boroughs in the outer, suburban parts of Greater London. A borough like Bromley, for example, already covers a considerable area and is therefore faced with bigger problems of access and communication than a more compact and centrally placed borough like Hackney.

Constitutionally, the new authorities in London do not differ from local authorities elsewhere in the country; they operate similar committee and departmental structures; and are composed of aldermen and councillors who give their services free. It could be argued that although the authorities in Greater London differ somewhat in the nature of their functions from authorities elsewhere, they are essentially performing local-authority functions and should therefore be treated no differently from other authorities.

The argument is valid as applied to the London boroughs, which do resemble more closely authorities in other parts of the country. But the G.L.C., because it plays a different role in an area containing far more people than any other local authority, occupies a rather

ambiguous position. On the one hand, the G.L.C. councillor is
concerned with a smaller range of functions than his counterpart in,
say, Birmingham; on the other, the problems he has to deal with are
in some ways more difficult simply because of the sheer size of
London and the place it occupies in our national life. It does not
follow that the chairman of a major G.L.C. committee necessarily
has a greater burden, or that there is a stronger case that he should
receive payment for his services. But there is surely a case for examining whether the G.L.C., as at present constituted, is best fitted to
undertake the tasks which it has been set. The G.L.C. itself, as was
described in an earlier chapter, has recently reorganised its committee
structure. This is important so far as it goes, but it does not really
answer the question; it is more in the nature of a modification of
what is basically still a conventional local-government structure.
Perhaps the time to examine this question will arise if and when
reform of local government outside Greater London is undertaken.
It will then be clear whether the government of Greater London is
to be a model for other areas or whether it is to remain unique. In
either case, this would be a good opportunity to review both the
constitution and the area of the G.L.C. and the London boroughs.

In summing up the working of the new system perhaps the main
note should be one of modest but cautious optimism. As far as the
G.L.C. is concerned, fears were expressed before it was set up that:

'this new authority seems all too likely to find itself ground between
the millstones of "borough primacy" and close Government supervision. Will the Greater London Council really be able to initiate
major new policies, or will it function as a sort of ghostly middleman
between town hall and Whitehall?'[1]

The G.L.C. is far from being a ghostly middleman. Yet there are
doubts whether in some respects it may prove to have too little
power and the boroughs too much. The weaknesses of the
Greater London Development Plan, for example, spring partly, it is
true, from the G.L.C.'s desire to work in harmony with the boroughs;
but in part they reflect the fact that the 1963 Act did not give the
G.L.C. overriding power to prepare a strategic plan for Greater
London. In housing, too, though perhaps to a lesser extent, the
G.L.C. may find it difficult, without specific powers, to secure
sufficient co-operation from the outer London boroughs to help in
meeting the more pressing needs of the inner boroughs. In traffic and
highways, on the other hand, the G.L.C. does not on the whole lack

[1] Peter Self: 'The Herbert Report and the Values of Local Government'
(*Political Studies*, X, 2, June 1962), p. 158.

adequate powers and the same is broadly true of its newer responsibilities for public transport. Here its achievements are at the moment potential rather than actual. Nor must it be overlooked that much of what the G.L.C. is attempting to do could not have been done at all under the pre-1965 system of local government in Greater London.

GREATER LONDON AND THE REST OF THE COUNTRY

At the time it was instituted in 1965, the new system of local government in Greater London had no counterpart elsewhere in the country. This is still the position, although if the Redcliffe-Maud Commission's proposals for the metropolitan areas of Merseyside, 'Selnec' and the west Midlands are accepted, these areas will have a local government structure resembling that in Greater London. Before considering the applicability of the London system elsewhere, we refer briefly to the one important service which has not been brought within the new system in Greater London, namely, the Metropolitan Police force.

The main argument in favour of bringing the Metropolitan Police under the control of the G.L.C. is that, as elsewhere in the country, they should be subject to some measure of local democratic control. Against doing so is the argument that the police function in London differs to such a degree from that in other parts of the country that it is more appropriate that it should be under direct central government control, with Parliament exercising democratic oversight.

The arguments are evenly balanced. The Metropolitan Police force is generally regarded as an efficient and well-run force. It seems doubtful whether transfer to local authority control would lead to any great improvement. On the other hand, there is the question of principle; that Londoners should be able to have some say in the running of a police force to which they contribute and which is there very largely for their protection. Against this is the fact that the Metropolitan Police does have special duties which are of a national character and are recognised in the payment of an additional grant from the central government. With the G.L.C. in existence, the present arrangements for the Metropolitan Police are more of an anomaly than they were formerly when there was no local authority whose area even approximated to that of the force. On balance, it is probably best that the arrangements should remain as they are.[1]

[1] It is worth remarking that the recent series of police force amalgamations has weakened the element of local authority control and to this extent the Metropolitan Police is not so anomalous.

We have argued that the new structure of local government set up by the 1963 Act does by and large offer the means of dealing with London's local government problems. It does not offer an ideal or complete answer; no system could. It raises doubts in some directions; and some of its potentialities may not be realised in practice. But on the whole the advantages outweigh the disadvantages. The question then naturally arises whether this system is to be regarded as something peculiarly adapted to London's needs, or whether it is capable, perhaps with modifications, of being applied elsewhere.

It should be stressed in the first place that this system was designed for London. If it were applicable elsewhere, one would expect that it might most easily be applied in those areas which have much in common with London—the large conurbations such as the west Midlands or south-east Lancashire. But although they have much in common, there are some striking differences. The most important is that other conurbations have a different character. Whereas London has grown from a single centre outwards, dominating the surrounding areas, and with no real rivals, the others have grown from the meeting of a number of distinct centres. They are true conurbations, in which the individual towns, although long since merged in a physical sense, still retain their individuality. Stockport and Salford are different from one another and from Manchester, even though the stranger might find it difficult to tell where one ended and the other began; and the same is true to a greater or lesser degree of Birmingham and Smethwick (now Warley) or Leeds and Bradford.

From a practical point of view, too, there would be difficulty in applying the London system elsewhere. Other conurbations tend to have one large centre and a number of smaller ones: Manchester in south-east Lancashire, Liverpool in Merseyside. A Greater Manchester with a series of 'Manchester Boroughs' would involve breaking up the existing Manchester into smaller areas for borough purposes. This would not be easy given the unified nature of the present city.[1]

There are other circumstances, too, partly accidental, which have perhaps made the London system more appropriate there than it would be elsewhere. London is wealthy, and even the smallest London borough has rateable resources sufficient for the effective perfor-

---

[1] The Redcliffe-Maud Commission, however, have proposed to retain Manchester intact as a 'metropolitan district' within a 'Selnec' metropolitan area, with the opposite disadvantage that it will then be more than twice as big as any other metropolitan district in the area, and over five times as big as the smallest (Warrington).

mance of its functions. This might not be true of authorities of a similar size elsewhere. Again, it follows from what has been said earlier that it is easier to regard Greater London as a unity than it might be for say south-east Lancashire.

But above all it must be remembered that the success of the London system depends on the achievement of a working balance between authorities which can only in part be written into Acts of Parliament. The remarkable degree of co-operation between the London boroughs, brought about in large part through the London Boroughs Association, did not result from statutory decree; but it contributes greatly to the easier working of the system. It also carries dangers the other way; that the boroughs may prove more powerful than the G.L.C. through their ability to combine. Thus to some degree it is also very much an experimental system. The G.L.C. has to carry out its role without dominating the boroughs but also without being dominated by them. Both represent legitimate interests which may sometimes be in conflict, but which rightly are institutionalised in the government of Greater London. It is not impossible that a similar system may be applied in the conurbations; but perhaps more likely that London, as so often in its history, will remain unique.

APPENDIX: THE LONDON BOROUGHS

Borough[1]	Constituent Authorities	Population[2]	Rateable value per Head[3] (£)
Barking (16)	Barking M.B. (major part) Dagenham M.B. (major part)	169,520	61
Barnet (30)	Finchley M.B. Hendon M.B. Barnet U.D. East Barnet U.D. Friern Barnet U.D.	316,240	71
Bexley (18)	Bexley M.B. Erith M.B. Crayford U.D. Chislehurst & Sidcup U.D. (northern part)	215,470	50
Brent (28)	Wembley M.B. Willesden M.B.	284,460	69
Bromley (19)	Beckenham M.B. Bromley M.B. Orpington U.D. Penge U.D. Chislehurst & Sidcup U.D. (southern part)	304,230	34
Camden (2)	Hampstead Met.B. Holborn Met.B. St Pancras Met.B.	231,680	141
Croydon (20)	Croydon C.B. Coulsdon & Purley U.D.	329,210	61
Ealing (27)	Acton M.B. Ealing M.B. Southall M.B.	298,720	78
Enfield (32)	Edmonton M.B. Enfield M.B. Southgate M.B.	267,830	68

187

Borough[1]	Constituent Authorities	Population[2]	Rateable value per Head[3] (£)
Greenwich (6)	Greenwich Met.B. Woolwich Met.B. 　(exc. N. Woolwich)	229,700	55
Hackney (4)	Hackney Met.B. Shoreditch Met.B. Stoke Newington Met.B.	243,180	59
Hammersmith (11)	Fulham Met.B. Hammersmith Met.B.	197,590	66
Haringey (31)	Hornsey M.B. Tottenham M.B. Wood Green M.B.	245,270	54
Harrow (29)	Harrow M.B.	208,220	57
Havering (15)	Romford M.B. Hornchurch U.D.	252,290	48
Hillingdon (26)	Uxbridge M.B. Hayes & Harlington U.D. Ruislip-Northwood U.D. Yiewsley & West Drayton 　U.D.	236,990	73
Hounslow (25)	Brentford & Chiswick M.B. Heston & Isleworth M.B. Feltham U.D.	205,580	81
Islington (3)	Finsbury Met.B. Islington Met.B.	241,890	78
Royal Borough of 　Kensington & 　Chelsea (12)	Chelsea Met.B. Kensington Met.B.	210,720	124
Royal Borough of 　Kingston upon 　Thames (23)	Kingston-upon-Thames 　M.B. Malden & Coombe M.B. Surbiton M.B.	144,480	70
Lambeth (9)	Lambeth Met.B. Wandsworth Met.B. 　(eastern part)	329,250	60
Lewisham (7)	Deptford Met.B. Lewisham Met.B.	281,140	43
Merton (22)	Mitcham M.B. Wimbledon M.B. Merton & Morden U.D.	184,220	62
Newham (17)	East Ham C.B. West Ham C.B. Barking M.B. (small part) Woolwich Met.B. (N. 　Woolwich)	255,130	57

Borough[1]	Constituent Authorities	Population[2]	Rateable Head[3] value per (£)
Redbridge (14)	Ilford M.B. Wanstead & Woodford M.B. Dagenham M.B. (small part) Chigwell U.D. (southern part)	246,090	52
Richmond upon Thames (24)	Barnes M.B. Richmond M.B. Twickenham M.B.	177,130	62
Southwark (8)	Bermondsey Met.B. Camberwell Met.B. Southwark Met.B.	293,120	63
Sutton (21)	Beddington & Wallington M.B. Sutton & Cheam M.B. Carshalton U.D.	165,430	59
Tower Hamlets (5)	Bethnal Green Met.B. Poplar Met.B. Stepney Met.B.	192,250	76
Waltham Forest (13)	Chingford M.B. Leyton M.B. Walthamstow M.B.	236,900	50
Wandsworth (10)	Battersea Met.B. Wandsworth Met.B. (western part)	321,720	49
City of Westminster (1)	City of Westminster Met.B. Paddington Met.B. St Marylebone Met.B.	243,960	415

NOTES:

The boroughs, together with the City of London and the Temples (population 4,210), comprise the area of Greater London for which the G.L.C. is responsible. The population of this area is (mid-1968) 7,763,820, with a rateable value (at April 1, 1967) of £646,030,871 (£82 per head).

The gross expenditure of the boroughs in 1966–7 was £458 million (£272 million net) and their total employees (June 1967) 217,278. Corresponding figures for the G.L.C. and I.L.E.A. combined are:

Gross expenditure £259 million (£141 million net)
Total employees 112,645

(*Source:* 1967 *Annual Abstract of Greater London Statistics*, Table 1.01, published by the G.L.C.)

[1] Numbers in brackets indicate the boroughs as listed in London Government Act, 1963, Schedule I, Part I.
[2] Registrar-General's Population Estimates, mid-1968.
[3] At April 1, 1968 (from *Municipal Year Book*, 1969).

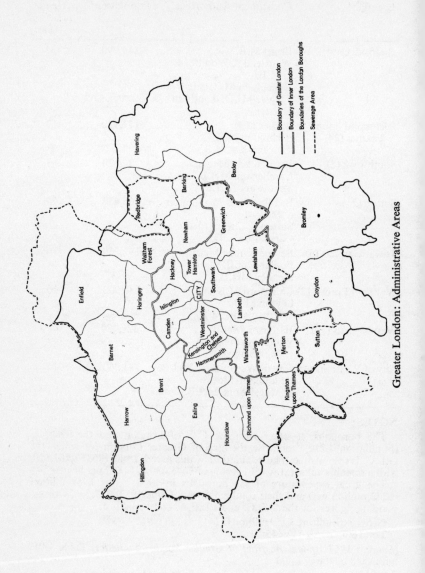

Greater London: Administrative Areas

INDEX

191

N

Acts of Parliament Cited

1829   Metropolitan Police Act
1835   Municipal Corporations Act
1855   Metropolis Management Act
1888   Local Government Act
1899   London Government Act
1902   Metropolis Water Act
1924   London Traffic Act
1933   London Passenger Transport Act
1936   Public Health (London) Act
1945   Water Act
1947   Transport Act
1952   Town Development Act
1963   London Government Act
1967   Local Government (Termination of Reviews) Act
1967   London Government Act
1969   Transport (London) Act
1969   Transport (London) Amendment Act

Commissions and Committees

1833   Royal Commission on Municipal Corporations
1854   Royal Commission on the City Corporation
1894   Royal Commission on the Amalgamation of City and County of London
1921   Royal Commission on Local Government in and around London (Ulls-water Committee)
1957   Royal Commission on Local Government in Greater London (Herbert Committee)
1962   Royal Commission on the Police
1967   Royal Commission on Local Government in England and Wales (Redcliffe-Maud Committee)

1945   Committee on number, size, boundaries and functions of Metropolitan Boroughs (Reading Committee)
1948   London Water Supplies Committee
1949   London Planning Administration Committee
1965   Housing in Greater London Committee (Milner Holland Committee)
1967   Management of Local Government Committee (Maud Committee)
1968   Committee on Local Authority and Allied Personal Social Services